A Drink at
JOEL'S PLACE

A Drink at JOEL'S PLACE

by Jess Moody

WORD BOOKS WACO, TEXAS

Affectionately dedicated . . .

  to my wife,
    my children,
    and my friends
    —without whom
    I would be a stranger

Foreword

As a layman who wants to like the church but doesn't understand what it is talking about, here is a cup of cold water in a desert of religious dust.

As a person whose life is communications, I see the church as a group of theologians talking to each other while the lay people and the "outsiders" are ignored—and too often want to be.

Into this situation strides a happy Christian minister who thinks the thoughts of Christianity but speaks so anybody —even I—can know the score in the only game the outcome of which *really* counts.

Surely not everybody will like this book. If they did, Jess Moody would rewrite it.

You may have detected that I am not an ardent fan of the church. Frankly, I'm not. I have yet to be convinced that the church as it is today is the one for which Christ died.

I think most churches need fumigation more than anything else.

This book is not the whole answer but it is the finest aroma I've gotten a whiff of in a long time.

An outsider can come to believe that preachers and church leaders are in an international conspiracy against fun. The thing Moody has done for the world is laugh with it instead of scowling at it.

While I am still quite skeptical about many things concerning Christianity, this book makes me *want* to believe it. I may not believe it all but Dr. Moody does and it *seems* to have made a ministerial Beau Geste out of him.

He doesn't have a Jimmy Cagney swagger about him but he is downright convinced and overjoyed about it.

Jess Moody would rather be dead than boring.

He isn't.

This man deliberately refuses to speak from the same frame of reference of any minister I know.

If what he is saying in this book had been said and heeded fifty years ago, the church would not be so ignored as it is today.

I hope teenagers will read this book—if they do they will never be the same.

Every adult, especially those of an almost completely pagan orientation like mine, must see this book. It will rattle them.

Every churchman ought to read it to learn how to dialogue with those on the outside.

Every sourpuss should read it to sweeten him up.

Every mixed-up person, which is most of us, ought to read it and reread it.

What I am saying is that this is a book for everybody but those with a completely closed mind.

CHET PIKE, JR.
Vice President
Scripps Howard

10

Preface

The world is as it is.

No matter how we romanticize it, decorate it, analyze it or criticize it—it is as it is.

The minister is as he is.

No matter how we romanticize him (a la Peter Marshall), decorate him (with ecclesiastic garb and symbols), analyze him (as Peale and his Peale-ings), or criticize him (with Sinclair Lewis' autobiography *Elmer Gantry*)—he is as he is.

I am a minister, of a sort.

I have romanticized my role, imagining myself to be now Martin Luther, now John Wesley, and now Dwight L. Moody.

I have decorated my body with ecclesiastical habiliments, my mind with a fetish for words or unique thought-patterns, and my attitude with sometimes phony love gush.

I have analyzed myself as Pastor, parent, adult, and child —and never admitted, even to myself, my findings.

I have criticized myself when I didn't mean a word of it; and, on most rare occasions, when I did.

And yet . . .

        . . . I remain as I am.

I have an ego.

Having read somewhere that a minister must be self-effacing, I fell into the same error of most ecclesiastics: I shot at me, cursed me, denied me, deprived me—and ended up sick of a losing battle. This resulted in lying to the public, criticizing my fellow frustrates, and being cynical about Christianity.

It was then that I made peace with the face I shave each morning. While reading the Gospels, I discovered that Christ did not want my ego dead—he wanted it to be his. So, I gave the battered, sick thing to him. He patched and polished it up, gave it a new motor, returned it to me and told me to live with it and that I couldn't live without it.

Since then I have been my own man and the whole thing has been sheer pleasure.

If you like this philosophy, I commend you for seeing things my way. If not, pray for me now and in the hour of my death.

I have glands.

All my life I have been told not to pay attention to such things. This is like living in Colorado Springs and ignoring Pike's Peak. My parents, very non-Victorian, always acknowledged glands as a reality. When I gave my life to the ministry, the church told me my glands really weren't there, to ignore them as one would the village idiot.

I had to choose between what my parents told me and what the learned church fathers had to say about it. Dad and Mother had a very limited education while the great white fathers had as many degrees as a sauna bath.

I ignored the pesky little things (glands, not the great white fathers!) for years, privately ogling and leering, publicly lying, all the while biting my fingernails to the elbow.

Then I discovered that Dad, Mother, and Jesus had been right all the time. What the Lord wanted me to do was have a happy family life and sublimate the residue of my vitality into joyous apostolic zeal.

Since that discovery, a good time has been had by all—except those who delight in spying out Christian liberty and accusing these happy souls of "antinomian excess." So, in order to further complicate an understanding of this book, let me hasten to state I do not believe in "antinomianism," whatever that is.

I am, as was said of Dr. Eric Berne, "a Freudian dropout" and a Christian drop-in.

I am as I am, as I said before.

Understanding the above denuding of the soul, one can begin to see that this volume will be as honest as I can make it, as inconsistent as I am, and no more or less believing or cynical than myself.

Whatever your final opinion of *A Drink At Joel's Place*, be assured that it is an effort at candid speech to give a spiritual shove to what I honestly believe to be a semi-neurotic church.

If the readers reject the book, I can console myself with the fact that I have a beautiful wife and a big church—thank God it isn't the other way around.

If there is enough reaction to it, I can always shine shoes in the square at Santa Fe or be the manager of a religious book nook in Las Vegas.

Until then, remember:

> "It is not whether
> You win or lose
> But . . .
> How much."
>
> —Jess Moody

Table of Contents

15

CHAPTER I

A Drink At
Joel's Place

The church has been concerned because the world isn't impressed with us and will not sit up and take notice.

The world won't sit up and take notice because we haven't sat up and taken notice of that which makes the world sit up and take notice.

The church needs to be informed that the world isn't obligated to pay any attention to us. I am convinced that they will when we deserve to be heard. We must merit an audience.

We are a church. The name church implies God. God means miracle. If we say we are a church and we cannot come up with a miracle, they think we are phony.

Maybe they are correct. If the only success they see in us is that which can be explained in terms of organization and management—that is, something the world could do with the same expenditure of effort and technique, they will one day finally repudiate us.

So, we must provide The Miracle or we have no justification for being.

. . . and no right to expect anyone to pay any attention to us.

Let us deserve to be heard and we will be.

What kind of miracle will cause the world to sit up and take notice?

The miracle of a different and better fellowship.

How superior is the fellowship at the church to that of two old friends fishing?

. . . or playing golf?

How much better is the sense of enjoyment among the saints to that of a well-organized country club? Can an average man *really* find more compassionate understanding at his church than he can at Joe's Bar? Is his pastor as willing to listen as a bartender?

Right at this point most Christians go blind and jump the track. They evade the question by moralizing, "The average man has no business comparing the church to a bar or a country club!"

The big fact is that, protest as we might, he *does* make the comparison.

Or we might complain, "He has no business being in Joe's Bar!"

John Q. Pagan then hitches up his belt and proceeds to show us he has not only the right to go there but the desire. In fact his desire will have been increased because he mutters, "At least *there* nobody sits in judgment on you!"

Thus the church's out-of-touchness is again emphasized.

What does John Q. find in a bar that he doesn't find in a lukewarm church?

Enjoyment, for one thing. Plain old-fashioned fun.

Here the average Christian jumps the track again. "The church wasn't put into the world to have fun."

I'll have to disagree with that Victorian judgment.

Fun was one of the chief characteristics of the apostolic church. "Hilarious" was a New Testament adjective used to describe the saints . . . and this concerned the giving of offerings to the Lord. Taking the collection is one of the low ebbs of a worship service. If *hilarious* describes a low ebb, they must have torn the house down when something exciting happened.

A proper interpretation of the Sermon on the Mount will indicate that there were several laugh lines in it. Orientals always respond to exaggerations-for-emphasis. This was Jesus' most effective speech instrument. The "camel through a needle's eye" approach brought gales of laughter in the first century.

Even today, any capable speaker knows the effectiveness of humor as a carrier belt of listener interest.

The early church sat loose in the saddle, made fun of death, giggling under their breath that they knew Something others didn't know about the Grim Reaper. That was the fact that his scythe could only kill the least important part of them—their temporary bodies. The whole thing was a tremendous Joke on the devil and Christian laughter rang out in the Circus Maximus and echoed in the catacombs.

To them, all heaven had broken loose through Jesus' victory on the cross. In the cross, God had played a Cosmic Trick on death. The devil laughed when our Lord went to the cross—then wept when he discovered why Jesus went there.

One wave after another of joyous Christian laughter washed upon the shores of time and finally caved in the Roman house of sand.

If the modern church could only break out in peals of thunderous laughter at communism, secularism, pseudo-scientism and vague relativism, the foundations of Satan's seriousness would crumble again.

All of the above listed temporary systems can cope with surface problems but none of them can remotely touch the deepest problems of man: sin, sorrow, and death.

Christ adequately answers these questions and this fact is God's most tremendous Joke.

Another experience the modern pagan finds in a bar that he cannot find in an unspiritual church is *fellowship*.

The modern, thinking Christian has been fed a rather sterile spoonful of philosophical pablum concerning fellowship.

Some vague paragraphs about *koinonia* as a beloved community have been ground out of the theological hopper but there seems to be little saving salve in it.

The idea of all the fellows being in the same ship might give the image of a surface unity but it heals nobody. The fellowship of a church family is not measured by how unanimously they support the preacher or a program, but by how many sick souls get cured.

Many churches have evolved a method by which everybody gets along with everybody else *inside* the family. But what about *The Outsider* who quivers in real pain and looks to see if there is a Balm in Gilead?

The secret of successful evangelism is for the word to leak out that spiritual blisters are healed at the church house. A veritable army of sinners will batter down the church's front door if it becomes the House Where Love Lives.

Publicans and sinners didn't give a hoot about the unity

of the Pharisees and the Sanhedrin, but they thronged the road and raised the roof to get near Jesus. Wherever Jesus is, there will always be a clamoring throng. Empty churches mean the Lord isn't near the place.

John Q. has the haunting suspicion that if he brought his troubles to the church his sin would be frowned on and gossiped throughout the village.

It is utterly amazing that most barkeepers are also excellent secret keepers.

They also offer Mr. Guiltspiller a whole lot of understanding and acceptance.

The one fact secularists seem to understand is that the church has never comprehended the difference between talking about love and *being* love.

That is, being understanding and acceptance.

When Mary Magdalene gave her heart away to Jesus, He didn't demand to see her identification papers.

She was understood and accepted and her only credential was that she provided the sinner.

Then He provided the Saviour.

Still another feature a bar provides is *anonymity and an opportunity for a man to be left alone, if he chooses.*

The barkeep detects that a man doesn't want to talk and immediately his wish is granted.

One of the surprises a new church member discovers is that he is deluged with offers of "opportunities of service."

This is like asking a newborn baby to drive a Mack truck.

Any person who has just entered into the radical reorientation brought about by the New Birth is, like Paul, in need of the quietude of an Arabian exile. The deeper meaning of what has happened to him must be explored. He must reappraise his relationship to God, man, and the universe and this cannot be done by a man who is Running Real Hard.

Service to God is a growth process—not a track meet with a "Let's set a new record next Sunday" complex.

Continually running the church treadmill builds a Christian who is all legs and no brain or heart.

We have reversed the process—it is the heart that makes the legs go—not vice versa.

We have been told of pagan worshippers who offer up their newborn to their gods. Could it be that the Christians of the latter part of the enlightened twentieth century do the same thing?

Haven't we witnessed the laying of some young Isaac on the altar of the church program ego? And unfortunately there is no lamb caught in the thicket.

One final feature about a bar is that *it provides the intoxication it advertises.*

A bar is always true to its name. When a customer comes in, they don't inform him that the only thing they serve is warm milk. If they were to do this, as many barflies would stay away from Joe's Bar as church members stay away from Sunday worship.

The church had better come up with the choicest product brewed at Joel's Place, called "This is That."

"This is that which was spoken by the prophet Joel; . . . it shall come to pass in the last days . . . I will pour out of my Spirit upon all flesh." Acts 2:16-17.

Let us cease being congregations of grey-flanneled countenances lest millions of John Q. Pagans bid us "Exit."

The bar has become the church of the secular city.

The church must provide more enjoyment, better fellowship, anonymity, and the intoxication it advertises . . . or start packing.

CHAPTER 2

How To
Unscramble An
Egg

We must understand the joy of rioting in His love and reveling in happy reverence.

The corset of regimented religion asks too much surrender of personhood, binding the buoyancy out of us.

There are too many staves of strictness that smack of purging pharisaism!

Hyper-legalism makes flatfooted people try to pirouette like a ballerina, resulting in spiritually unflattering postures.

Educated icebergs, having no heart, forfeit the right to lead men from being promotional protagonists into attractive piety.

You aren't converting men if your only mission is to drive the cattle-people through some semi-sanctified dipping vat. They'll all end up in the slaughter house and hate you for it.

A baptized biped without the New Birth is a captured saphead who is utterly incapable of caring for himself.

No man is spiritually changed, evangelized, until he can hustle his own Gospel groceries.

I pray that one by one the foolish interpretation of evangelism too many of us hold will fall away like overripened pears.

God give us Christians in long trousers who can bake their own bread.

Strip us of fad following and rubber-stamp respectability.

Give us some good, brewing in our brains, that can hang on when the emotion of our first decision has worn off.

We will win the world when we realize that fellowship, not evangelism, must be our primary emphasis. When we demonstrate the Big Miracle of Love, it won't be necessary for us to go out—they will come in.

This will eliminate our pathetic reliance upon preaching to win people. Epileptic jawbones, the perpetual motion machines upon which we have too long relied, have done nothing but generate cyclones.

No one has ever been blown into the Kingdom of God.

Men aren't won by wind.

Men are won by Jesus Christ.

It is my belief that it is almost impossible to reject Christ —if He is seen as He really is.

Not a scowling Saviour or dour Judge . . .

. . . or, as Ibsen's Julian called Him, "The Prince of Renunciation."

This misinterpretation has produced some myopic misanthropes who, wearing the corset too tightly, walk about with their bloodshot eyes bulging and call it the Christian demeanor.

Joan of Arc was burned but these mock martyrs are squeezed to death.

It is a tragedy when one has to check the rule book to find out when to smile.

Not only are they miserable in the corset but they want to put you in it also. That is too many people in one corset.

They frown themselves out of the right to witness.

If they hear someone who, in a fit of feisty fidgets, says "shucks" it pains these holy ones and their faces register the protest.

When a Sure Enough Sinner, bristling with rambunctiousness and rebellion, emits a string of virile and unique theological terms, it hospitalizes these Choked Ones for two weeks.

How unlike Jesus whose loving face broke the heart of a cursing ex-fisherman in the midst of his denials.

How unlike Jesus who discovered good where others saw only evil—in cheap politicians, nymphomanic divorcees (the Woman at the Well), and a thief twisting in death agony on a Roman gibbet.

His capacity for sympathetic understanding of the wretched estate of People-Really-Shook-Up-by-Sin is as measureless as space.

To Him, people and their needs superseded rules. He shattered Sabbath regulations to quench the hunger of men.

What difference did it make if some man-made regulations were splintered, if a withered hand was made supple, and a frosted psyche melted?

The church must cease thinking itself so divine that it refuses to join the human race.

Jesus was not an Essene, bowing out of the family of man to live in solitary confinement.

He identified with the shepherd and the fisherman (Luke 5:1-11; John 10:1-16; Matthew 25:31-46; and Luke 15:3-7).

He knew the life of the carpenter and the gardener (Luke 8:6-9; Matthew 7:16-21; 24-26).

He could hobnob with pearl salesmen and housewives (Matthew 8:33-34).

He could carry on an animated conversation with a vine dresser (Matthew 20:22, Matthew 20:1-16; John 15:1-10).

He could have a ripping good discussion with a tailor (Mark 2:21).

Jesus would never attend a rush party for the Quad Sigs, the Sacred Sorority for Snubbing Sinners.

Neither would He have broken His identification with nature.

He took life and romped with it—all of life, all of nature.

So many church people act as though the world is an insult and they'll be getting out of it as soon as they can book passage.

They sing, "This world is not my home—I'm just passing through," or "I am a poor wayfaring stranger . . . a long way from home."

Jesus would never have tolerated such an attitude. He thoroughly enjoyed every beautiful living thing about the world He lived in.

He examined natural phenomena, and closely.

When he spoke, he didn't resort to high-blown theological expression. Words like *eschatology, existential,* and *vicario-vital* never fell from His lips. He was no non-communicative ice block.

He always spoke to the people sitting directly in front of Him, not to some invisible, non-existent coterie of theologs.

Like the seminary student speaking to a dozen farm folks from just out of Calhoun, Kentucky, saying, "Now, I know what you are thinking: 'That smacks of sabellianism.' "

Jesus would never get caught with His mind in neutral.

He would have warmed up that Kentucky audience by talking about wheat and tares being like the childen of Satan, and the birds gobbling up the seed before it sprouted. (Matthew 13:38).

His audience would have leaned forward when He told them about God's attitude toward a little dead bird, lying frozen in the morning cold (Matthew 6:26).

They would have comprehended every word He said when He told them the sun shines on the skinflint as well as the saint (Matthew 5:44, 45).

The poor people would have had fresh inspiration sweep across their faces when Jesus told them that God cared about what the well-dressed lilies would be wearing this season (Matthew 6:28-30).

Those farmers would have understood what the dear Lord meant when He spoke about the mystery of where the wind comes from and where it goes (John 3:8).

Every pew would become an electric chair when Jesus spoke of a seed germinating and growing until the full corn appears in the ear (Mark 4:27).

To Jesus, who was always comfortable in any environment, this world was His home; and in spite of the fact that He was just passing through, He drank the nectar of this earth's nature.

After twenty centuries, isn't it time the church learned from Jesus that a strong identification with this world's comprehension is essential to good witnessing? But how does such identification come about?

It is said that Hal Holbrook spends three and a half hours getting into Mark Twain's makeup and spent 13 years getting into Mark Twain's psyche.

A Christian might spend three and a half hours preparing a talk about Christ but it takes a lifetime to get into Jesus' psyche.

Only the Christ life can unscramble the egg of a crazy mixed-up id.

The spatula that performs this spiritual wonder of unscrambling is conformity to the image of Jesus Christ.

The American technique of bringing about "success" in accomplishing this quest for the whole man through the Christ life is usually the pursuit of bigness.

If it is large and effective, it simply must be good.

This sort of quantitative religion has set back the true faith by two hundred years.

Samuel Coley says, "The essence of a circle lies in its roundness, not its bigness."

The essence of the Christ life is its spirituality, not its size, number, or distance.

It is not our gargantuan proportions but gospel conformity that determines our inner peace with God.

We are a success only when we can live without success.

Our salvation comes not by works but by grace that produces works.

Only one work that really matters is possible for us— when the battle was blackest and the time for moral grandeur came, the future generations must be able to say we confessed His name.

I tell you—stand—and this mediocrity-molded, relativity-ridden age will find your faith irresistibly magnetic . . .

. . . and they will be drawn back to Melody.

O, God, the world needs to learn how to sing again.

Our age knows the words—may the Holy Spirit give back to us the music.

CHAPTER 3

The Death Of
Labels

A major denomination has been wrestling with a decision to change its name. This struggle has been spread over several years and has resulted in quite some activity on each side of the question.

In discussion of this matter with a man who has no umbilical cord with the church, he made one of the most profound comments I've heard:

"The people will go to the more magnetic centers of spirituality. Labels mean little these days."

His statements did not contain a tinge of acid and a taste of bitters but was spoken right out of the middle of the mouth without the batting of an eye.

In spite of my tendency to bark out a half dozen amendments to his contention, his clear-eyed candor had hit home.

I felt the honesty and the truth of it.

My first temptation was to give a soft reply to his hard saying and proceed with the business of churchmanship.

But for quite a while later I was at my dismal worst due to an intriguing preoccupation with the teeth in his remark: "Labels mean little these days."

Inside of me the weight of custom was bucking the urgency of change. Couldn't I reach into my santified sack of semantics and shoot him down before he said anything like that again?

Or cover him up with a statistical baptism proving that the denomination could handle it all and Do the Job?

I could, but the stats haven't been too impressive the last few years.

He had fired a dum-dum into me—you know, the kind that doesn't explode until it gets into your head.

The thought keeps crowding me: What is a label?

A label is a promise of the quality of the product bearing it.

An item can be called "Gold" but if inside the package is pancake mix, the sales campaign will be as flat as the product and it won't even sell like hotcakes.

Kleenex is not an exact semantic definition of facial tissue, it is the title given to a certain brand of facial tissue.

Yet nine of ten people who order facial tissue say, "I want a box of Kleenex." The reason for this is that the label kept its promise. In fact, it kept its promise so well that facial tissue ceased being that and became Kleenex.

The same is true of Coca-Cola. I contend this product could have been called "Gook" and it would have sold just as well.

Coca-Cola doesn't sell well because of its name. It sells because it keeps its promise by appealing to more taste buds and making the quenching of thirst an occasion instead of a bodily function.

Keeping the name Coca-Cola will not make it sell any better; change the name and within six months it will sell just as well, if the product keeps its promise.

A label is not only the keeping of a promise, it is also a pledge to maintain the quality of the product.

If overnight the Kleenex people should decide to make their product of fine sandpaper, the public would start asking for facial tissue again.

If they determined to add to Coca-Cola just a dash of Grandma's Lye Soap, there isn't a chart low enough to measure the sales drop.

Products that sell are those that maintain the quality year in, year out.

The death of a product is assured once the quality is cut.

This is true of a church or a denomination as well. Just because it has a religious name assures no sacredness or uniqueness to the institution.

Some have the idea that the product can be inferior simply because it is called Baptist or Presbyterian. They have the notion that the *label* will carry the institution.

In reality, the opposite is true. The institution must carry the label.

There isn't a man walking this earth who must follow a church out of respect *for that for which it once stood.*

It is not the community's obligation to protect and support the church; it is the church's obligation to protect and support the community.

It is the church's obligation to be Something Great Big for God and nobody owes it any allegiance if it is not.

Let the product weaken; and overnight, like Kleenex made of sandpaper, the demand will drop off . . .

. . . and should.

The key men to the church's ability to keep the promise to the public is the minister and the Really Concerned Layman.

I saw an old minister and his sweet companion of sixty years as they walked by our sun-kissed Chapel-by-the-Lake.

His story was most familiar to me.

He was an almost completely educated man in the art of character analysis and loving support.

He had been Mr. Valiant-For-Truth for six decades.

This now old man had sniffed, for the glory of God, the odors of poverty, despair, and sin . . .

. . . and sought to dispense grace where the beer and cockroaches play.

No one but the Little People knew he existed; but all his life he had battled a blasé Protestantism, challenging it to waken from its somnambulism.

He was greatness personified and I am sick of the modern novelists who depict him and his ilk as a naive nitwit of a moon-bloom who would flunk out of a class of morons.

I have seen, on rare occasions, the uncommitted clod who shares nothing and is nothing; who will not become involved in the sick, sad, sottish, sordid, sensate lives of people from whom he extracts the tithe, seeing humanity as bizarre figures in a puppet theatre.

But for every Elmer Gantry, the alias of Sinclair Lewis, there are a thousand Albert Schweitzers who can walk down Main Street with heads up, using their own names.

The early church was full of these dear, debonair, happy-in-Jesus saints who with loving, dying hands knew how to hold high the Light of the World when the chips were down.

One thing was certain.

Nero knew they were in town.

This bland, yawning age is quietly dedicated to putting as many nicks as possible in the cutting edge of prophecy.

The key to keeping the promise of the label is the preacher. He must be popular and prophetic.

His sermons should be highly spiced bite-sized snacks— the kind that feed people and keep them going.

He may make the mistake of serving a full intellectual meal. But he must remember, a meal is eaten a bite at a time.

If it is served in too large chunks, the people will get the holy hiccups.

The prophet-preacher must reflect what he really is—not what the rigid regimentarians say he should be. To witness a minister cut himself to the size, shape, and pace of the demands of the more neurotic elements of his congregation is a spectacle to make the angels ache.

To see a race horse pulling a plow is a pathetic picture exceeded only by seeing a plow horse in a race.

The plow horse in this particular metaphor is a dogmatic, ambiguous, and outmoded bumpkin preaching in an age of the race to Mars.

This type goes over much like the fabled high jumper who is eight months pregnant.

We must understand that the earth has never been shaken by nice little talks about divinity.

The sermons don't have to be gutsy but they do have to be characterized by courage.

This courage will be brought into play again when the sleep walkers react to such hard-hitting sermons.

Such a minister must be ready to lose some popularity.

I never heard a true prophet introduced as a distinguished and thoughtful minister.

But the Big Test comes when the sermon gets the accolade

of the best part of your redeemed nature, causing it to stand up and cheer. When that happens you can rest assured there will be demonic reaction to it.

The surest way to defeat is for the minister to take this reaction seriously, to pout, lick his bruises, and nurse his bitternesses.

There will always be those friends of Job who will be delighted to tell you "One more sermon like that and you'll be wiped out."

If your best nature liked your sermon and the whole world hates it, tell them all to go to heaven—and begin preparing another sermon just like the other one, only better.

But beware, a man can be tempted to compromise. He who resists this temptation will one day find the applause of the angels to be deafening.

The label never suffers under this sort of product.

Every man on earth is somehow crippled by sin. It is the Christian's job to carry one corner of this man's blanket in cooperation with other Christians who carry the other corners in order to get the crippled man to Jesus.

Laymen who cannot crack a Greek diphthong or administrate a church the size of a supermarket can provide the one missing ingredient the church needs most—they can carry one corner of the blanket.

"I went to a church office," a broken man told me, "and I found information, wintry efficiency, a dozen garbled theological expressions, and a methodical prayer. I was given a God-bless-you, a religious tract, and the front door. I went out into the street just as I had come in from it—frustrated, sick of sin, and afraid. They gave me everything but the one thing I needed—help."

A young lady, a new convert to Christianity, came to a

national denominational convention. She had been highly successful in business and now she wanted to enter some phase of full time, church-related Christian activity.

Let her tell her own story.

"I came to Detroit expecting to see ministers walking arm in arm, with happiness written on every face. I expected the predominant question to be 'How can we further our great fellowship and how can we communicate the Gospel?'

"What I found has almost devastated my spiritual wonder. I have seen men in 'secular' conventions more motivated for money than these men were motivated for God and love. These preachers are an army of insecurity, marching to the tune of mediocrity, and packing the deadweight of rifles that fire only blanks. These 'soldiers' don't even know who the enemy is.

"They hate a successful pastor more than they do the devil. I came seeking help and ended up giving aid. I think there are those with courage enough to try to solve the problem; but, beware, it could cost them everything.

"I'm trying to piece my life together after this shattering experience. The only thing I have left is a dynamic experience with Christ. I'm sure that's all I need."

Is there an honest soul who can deny the validity of this young lady's complaint?

We cannot publically talk of brave new ventures in evangelism and privately cut down our fellow troops.

This is the Giant Hypocrisy of our time.

We cannot carry one corner of a broken world's sin so long as we emphasize evangelism without fellowship.

In fact, a strong case can be made that the church should not primarily emphasize evangelism. The church in the Book of Acts was basically a radiating fellowship.

If the Christian public can convince the world that in this age of duplicity, double-dealing, and almost scientific skulduggery, there is one body of people who can be trusted, where mutual respect is a daily reality, and there is real honest fun among them; if, I say, this can be solidly conveyed to the world, evangelism of the proportions of Pentecost will be the result.

People don't go where the action is, they go where Love is.

But if the Love be a many-splintered thing, they will avoid it like the plague, no matter how evangelistic we may be.

We know of split churches that are highly evangelistic. They are a dime a dozen and worth not half that much.

When will we realize that we are to be a House of Help to the Man Outside?

I am referring to simple forms of help . . .

. . . like the young actress helping a demented woman into the baptismal waters of the Chapel-by-the-Lake . . .

. . . like the young athlete reading to a blind friend,

. . . like the lawyer's wife baking a cake for a bereaved family . . .

. . . like the young florist leaving his work to assist an elderly tourist whose husband had dropped dead . . .

. . . like a tired minister sitting up the rest of the night to try to reconcile a divided home.

It is this love for areas other than the soul that causes the soul to Come Across.

But the brutal truth is that we offer a theoretical plan of salvation instead of a Living Way.

This is why congregations listen like bored mules hitched to Studebaker wagons, flicking flies.

Too often we've acted like the neighborhood scold who leads in meditation about other people's sins.

May God forgive our churches for being in too healthy a state of tidiness. It is the House of the Holier-Than-Thou and no fellowship, a Big Bunch of Bible Bangers.

To find lasting happiness in such a place is as frustrating as being a match in an asbestos factory!

There is no use trying to forge a spiritual democracy out of eighteen different tribes of ecclesiastical cannibals we laughingly call a congregation.

Our factions speak louder than words.

This is why the world won't allow us to speak to them— they have enough problems without our compounding them.

If we are as sick, as critical, as divided as they, we will never be asked to carry a corner of their blanket.

Our performance may be Barrymore-ish but it will be done offstage. The masses never cheer or follow an understudy.

When the church is told to stand in the wings while Science and Government perform onstage before the world's population, you know full well . . .

. . . that church labels are dead.

Roy Gustafson has distilled the very essence of the only means by which the church can find the road back.

"The Holy Spirit never gathers to a denomination. He never gathers to an ordinance. He never gathers to a doctrine. He never gathers to a ritual. The Holy Spirit of God always gathers to the Person of Christ. The very moment we are born of God's Word and God's Spirit, we are immediately joined to Christ. Regardless of how sincere a soul winner may be, he cannot add one member to the body of Christ. It would be like putting wax apples on a tree. The Holy Spirit alone does the work."

To repeat, "The people will go to the more magnetic centers of spirituality. Labels mean little these days."

CHAPTER 4

Peace

John Edmund Haggai, in his book *How To Win Over Worry*, tells the story of a Mrs. Monroe of Darlington, Maryland. She was the mother of eight children. One day, Mrs. Monroe came home from the grocery and saw five of her children intensely interested in something.

Closer observation terrified her as she saw that they were playing with several cute little skunks.

She screamed at the top of her voice, "Children, run!"

. . . and each kid grabbed a skunk and ran!

Her frantic scream frightened them so much that they squeezed the skunks . . .

. . . and skunks simply do not like to be "squz."

In dealing with the subject, "Peace, Its Price and Prize," man has a subject which he can pick up and run with—and squeeze. Modern secularism has given forth with foul squeezings in offering pagan panaceas for peace.

Men want peace—desperately. A nagging wife wrote a number of letters of complaint to her soldier husband, fighting in Viet Nam. His answer is a classic: "Will you please stop writing those vicious letters so I can fight this war in peace?"

Men want peace—even in wartime.

When we say we want peace, for what are we asking? Until we define what we are looking for, it will be quite impossible to find it.

There is that peace which is the mere silencing of cannons. Some think complete peace has come when the great god of war slowly rises and closes his bloody book. Is this all we want and need in this life?

I heard about two bulldogs that fought every day. At the appointed hour for canine combat, these two would square off and fight until both were so exhausted that they just lay in the grass and growled at each other. The only peace they had was the peace resulting from exhaustion of the two combatants.

This is the only sort of peace this nation has known since our country was founded—the peace caused by the fact that we were too tired to fight.

And even during that peaceful time hate mongers feed coal to the lust for war by capitalizing for profit on man's unregeneracy. After they have done their dirty work, a murderous mania grips the minds of men. The pulse of the race sounds reveille. The soul of the nation flexes its muscles. Savagery is resurrected and we seem further than ever from that wondrous age.

The sensuous call for slaughter, the lust for blood is hot in the world. Twinkling cynically over Moscow and Washington the stars are evil, and hate, lunging hot from hell, sears the inner heart of every man.

This uncovered energy will find expression. Pent-up passions are ready to explode. Inflamed imagination hankers to hear the mad hiss of the bullet and the sickening crush of steel.

The natural man, untamed by Christ, is but an educated savage—ultimately his national meanness will demand its pound of flesh.

O, God in Christ, save us from the delusion that war is essential to scientific creativity. Save us from believing that heroes are forged only by the bloody sweat of Da Nang. Save us from believing that genius is the child of widow's tears. Teach us that one warlike generation regurgitates another just like it!

Hyper-dispensationalists have leavened us with the idea that there can be no peace—ever. But how do we know that? Have we ever really tried?

Every major nation on earth has a War Department. No nation on earth—anywhere—has a Peace Department.

I do not intend to sound like the pollyanna pacifists of a generation ago. They have done their damage by singing peace when there is no peace. By lulling this strong Samson, America, to sleep, while Delilah, the Devil himself, clipped our locks.

The liberal Protestants have painted our house white.

The hyper-fundamentalists with their leather lungs and no ethics have allowed the props to rot and the pillars cannot sustain our gilded roof.

You cannot have peace when a boasted civilization is breaking beneath its own ponderous weight.

Adlai Stevenson said, "A nation glued to the television screen, one that spends more than any other society has on drink and tranquilizers, one that spends more on advertising than education, that evades the rigors of creative activity and is indifferent to all but athletic excellence, one that enjoys the trivial and the mediocre, one committed to pleasure and profit alone—such a chaotic, selfish, indifferent, commercial society will be at a loss before the iron pioneers of the new collective society."

Perhaps we are seeking another sort of peace. We cannot deal with our problems so we whistle in the dark by seeking unconsciousness through martinis, the peroxide blonde, and potent pills.

It has been twenty-five years since Pearl Harbor, and 400,000 American deaths later, men still think they can find peace through tranquilizers.

Dr. R. G. Lee says, "If all the tranquilizers were taken from America, there would be such a national nervous breakdown that there would not be enough well people to take care of the sick people."

Or we seek peace by having men tell us we are really not so bad off.

At the American Baptist Convention two years ago, someone said, "The difference between the first century and the twentieth is that Paul was appealing while Peale is appalling." While I greatly love and respect Dr. Peale for his truthful preaching of the power of God in human life, I do not care for the little Peale-ings who pervert what he originally intended by saying, "A good time will be had by all if everybody will just look real glad."

And while we were looking real glad, smiling as though we were posing for a family portrait, somebody cut the innards out of this wonderful nation of ours.

And if we fall someone can read T. S. Eliot's epitaph for us, "And the winds shall say, 'Here lies a decent, godless people. Their only monument to civilization was an asphalt road and a thousand lost golf balls.' "

False prophets can damn us by preaching false peace.

Some preach justification as a legal fiction.

Some preach peace by denying hard reality.

Some preach sanctification when what they refer to is but the gradual dying of glands.

"The way of peace have they not known" (Romans 3:17).

Let us listen to the Man with nail-pierced hands as He tells a sick, sick, sick nation about His peace.

"Let not your hearts be troubled. I have overcome the world."

"My peace give I unto you: not as the world giveth, I give unto you."

Paul pointed to Jesus and said, "He is our peace."

I see the giant executioner with two large, square nails between his teeth, a crude hammer in his hand. His knee is cupped into the elbow pit of the carpenter from Nazareth. With his calloused fingers, the executioner feels the wrist of Jesus to find the little hollow spot. Then he drives the nail into the spot.

The executioner steps across the body to the other wrist.

The cross is raised and dropped into its place. The executioner nails the right foot over the left.

The crucified man, with his arms upstretched in V-fashion, feels unbearable pain in his wrists, and muscle cramps flame in his forearms, upper arms, and shoulders. The muscles in the sides of his chest ache with paralysis. It is possible to inhale but impossible to exhale.

This causes Jesus to repeatedly raise himself up to force the air from his lungs. Then, when strength is gone, he relaxes on the cross and inhales.

Jesus repeats this process again and again until it is almost impossible to raise himself.

Then using his last measure of strength to rise up just one more time, He shouts as He exhales, "It is finished!"

The Son of God slumps upon the cross . . . smothers to death.

This is our God, straining to the limit, in hatred for our sins.

This is our God shouting, "Either give up your sin—or give up hope!"

"He is our peace."

This is the price of peace.

I see a young man, pacing to and fro, wrestling with a habit pattern established during childhood.

I see a lovely young girl, smoldering with passion, not too sure it would be wrong to lower her moral standards in order to gain a measure of popularity.

I see a tweedy, corpulent, horn-rimmed dollar-chaser we sometimes call man. He is debating a choice between two roads: the right and the near right. Just a little withholding of information here and financial security will be his. Society will still respect him and he will be rich.

I see America's Tired Woman, the housewife. She thinks her family believes her to be nothing more than the scullery maid. She picks up here and straightens there. She finishes preparing one meal and sees that it is time to start another.

I see a big business man, in his executive suite, sitting behind a desk the size of a billiard table. He is surrounded by good looking secretaries, business charts, cigar smoke, and flattery. He is a twelve-cylindered, five-ulcered success.

I see an open-shirted, hairy-chested industrial worker, staggering home tired and exhausted. He is greeted by a hag of a nagging wife, a steaming house full of dirty kids. And he hurls himself out into the welcome cool air of the night—out into that neon wilderness, the human jungle, the forest of concrete until he ends up in a dimly lit chrome-plated, cushioned chaos of a bar. And after his sixth beer he slobbers out his sad story of inner sickness to a glassy-eyed peroxide sitting across from him, acting as though she is listening so he will buy her another beer.

What about these people?

What about these little heartbroken nobodies?

We have a word for them.

Let the mental know-it-alls laugh if they must.

Let the high churchmen make mock if they will.

Let them call it, "saw-dust trailism" if they want to.

Let the super aesthetes hold their noses and condescend-ingly call it, "The Old-Time Religion" if they must . . .

. . . But the answer to all broken-hearted men every-where is "Come to Jesus Christ!"

Jesus is both the Price and Prize of my peace.

CHAPTER 5

Me And My House

I grew up in West Texas. In fact, I evolved into adolescence near the culture center of the world—which is, as anybody knows, Muleshoe, Texas.

For no earthly reason my family always had a great deal of pride. I wondered at their infatuation with their genealogy, so I had my family tree looked up—then I had it hushed up.

While checking the family pattern, I discovered an uncle Zeke—he had more pride than anybody.

One day the village blacksmith was hammering a glowing red horseshoe. He happened to hit it a little awry and it fell into the dust near the door.

Just about that time, Uncle Zeke came in and saw the horseshoe which had just lost its reddened glow, but was still as hot as a depot stove.

Zeke reached down and picked up the horseshoe. Of course, he immediately threw it down.

"What's the matter, Zeke, is it hot?" laughed a group of onlookers.

Zeke raised his pride-filled self to his highest height and answered, "No, it just don't take me long to look at a horseshoe."

It didn't take me long to look at this subject to realize that it was a basic and a potentially boring one.

What do you say about the American Home that hasn't been said better and more often?

Don't you traditionally preach about the alarming divorce rate, the sad story of liquor and its contribution to the destruction of the home and the foundations that build a successful home?

So . . . since I am an addict of the status quo—as just about everybody else is—I intend to approach this great and needy topic in a typical way, yet at the same time to suggest some atypical approaches.

Oh, I could say that the foundation of the very structure of our security is the home.

But that platitude would not really shake or challenge us . . . we have heard it too often.

We must come to some solid convictions concerning the home and its importance, or our America will collapse.

I am no calamity-howler stating that the foundations are shaken . . . but have you noticed the little cracks in the ground? The churches have contributed to this very great problem in several ways.

For one thing, *I am convinced that most of us have, through some tragic misemphasis, been dusting the furniture while the house is on fire.*

I am not sure the church considers too many really fundamental issues.

We have our annual ecumenical-independent conflicts.
We go through the emotional orgy of the liberal-conservative tensions and settle most of those issues on the basis of
our glands instead of our brains.

But, when you get downright honest about the whole
situation, how many of our people know what we are talking about when we discuss Bishop Pike or the "God is
Dead" movement.

How many of our people know what "ecumenical"
means? Or care?

While we have wasted a generation in deciding who is
the most hot-blooded on which burning issue, a whole
stratum of our people have had their lives dashed on the
rocks because their homes have collapsed and we haven't
done much about it.

While we have resolved, resoluted, amended, and where-
as-ed, wrestling with theological issues, the seeds of which
were sown when we were seminary or college students, Bob,
Mary, Sally, and Billy have gone without any sure word
from the Lord concerning the heartbreaking disintegrating
of their little home.

My congregation looks up at me with such trust and respect that it terrifies me to realize that I cannot create a
program that will really help them to live together in spiritual rapport.

I can preach to them, rattling off reports of our growth,
inundating them with a statistical baptism, but I have the
feeling that my people go home on flat tires, having failed
again to find some help.

As Father Divine said one time, "Too many of us meta-
physicians don't know how to tangibilitate."

I know I don't when it comes to fathoming the neurotic

concretizing which has deadlocked some families into frozen islands of psychic frigidity.

It bombs me out to realize that here in predominately Protestant America, 50% of all the divorces of the entire world take place, and about 75% more are strongly tempted to break up.

When the chill of these facts blasts into my face, I realize that winter cannot be far behind.

There has never been a spring to follow a national spiritual winter.

Is America merely existing on the impetus of a godly ancestry? And when the force of that godly ancestry plays out, is America finished?

I don't know, but I do believe that these ecclesiastical sideshows will not help solve the basic heartbreak of the moral collapse of this country.

I want to make a frank admission: The denominational calendar and the church program have not contributed to the success of my own homelife. The success of my marriage has been the result of the great Christian patience of my wife and the sometimes sullen and grudging acquiescence of my precious children to the fact that "Daddy won't be home again tonight due to another church meeting—but we will sacrifice, won't we, children, because it is for the church."

No wonder so many preachers' children revolt.

Rebellious Baptist kids make excellent Episcopalians, they tell me.

This is a complete shattering of the image of the Pastor as the servant of the Lord and His church. It rather pictures us as the managers of a religious supermarket.

This could ultimately damn us to irrelevancy.

A church can be irrelevant just so long—then it will be repudiated.

When I consider the fact that my people were asked to attend more than 3,000 activities at my church last year, I shudder.

When I consider the fact that some of us have told our people that the more of these meetings they attend, the more spiritual they will be—I weep.

When I consider that my church could have observed 78 special weeks in the last 52, I think we are poor mathematicians if we try.

I must say this because I am as tired as the next man. I do wish we could cut our program in half so visitation and prayer will not be considered an intrusion.

How can this be done?

For one thing, can't some of our program be transferred to the home instead of being conducted at the church?

This would put more responsibility on the parents and cause more spiritual rapport between the members of the family?

You say the people won't do this?

My answer is: "They are not doing what we ask them to do now!"

They might as well not be doing it at home as not be doing it at the church . . . and some WILL do it and discover some golden moments of Christian love . . . at home.

Who says that all the church activities MUST take place at the church building? Why couldn't much of our program be transferred to home activity? Why could not a whole new curriculum for home study be encouraged? If we would sincerely get behind it and give it as much push as we give to other programs, it would be as successful as they are.

But I assure you it will not succeed at all unless we are
willing to drop several activities at the church.

It will fail unless we make it clear that church is the ally
—not the enemy—of the home. It will be frustrated unless
we convince the average church member that this will help
build his family into a greater spiritual unit.

We have missed a great point and it is costing us dearly.
We have emphasized individual faith with no relation to
any larger social unit. We have had emphasized an ecumenical faith with little reference to any smaller social unit.

America's great problems have not been solved by efforts
at individual evangelism or by collective denominational cooperation.

We have been fighting this ecumenical problem for well
over a generation.

Ecumenical Christianity has not solved our problems—
but, frankly, neither has Lone Rangerism remedied many
of them.

I want to level the charge that history may record that
America died because its spiritual wellsprings dried up due
to the fact that the churches were fighting over the wrong
issues. The biggest issue we face is not all this ecclesiastical
folderol . . . the gut issue is, what will the church do to
keep John, Mary, Billy, and Susie Doe lashed to the cross
and made into happy servants of the Lord Christ?

We must solve this depth problem. Our nation's President
stated that in the next 10 to 15 years, perhaps 20 nations
will be able to wage nuclear warfare.

Are those nations sophisticated enough, spiritual enough,
to handle such power? Hugh Downs says this will be like
"giving old-fashioned straight razors to a room full of kin-
dergarten children."

The President further stated: "Every man, woman, and child lives under the sword of Damocles. . . ."

I am deeply convinced that the thread that holds the sword is simply our answer to the question, "Will we be Christ-like and Spirit-filled?"

This is not naive oversimplification. The only way the message of Christ can change the world is by a contagious conflagration of Spirit-fire.

This can neither be done with programming nor without it. But it is most apparent that it cannot be done without a host of ignited human beings, with the Holy Spirit as the Flame.

The way to begin is to commence.

The Greeks solved their problems in the forum or the market place. The Hebrews solved their problems in the home, under patriarchal leadership.

The modern hope is for Christians to be more Hebrew than Greek.

But the modern father is too often a sad dad without teen-feel; an unromantic eunuch, whose total thought-patterns are "up at the office."

When he comes home, he is as loutish and insensitive as a baronial landlord, as remote as a maharajah.

He is a "martini-oiled mechanism," and little more.

He lives a busy, rich, empty life; he has lost his position of authority and leadership in the home and looks back longingly to the days when "they were more trouble free and less wrinkle prone."

Once their marriage was all golden. The young couple looked at each other like gilded mooncalves. They leaned against each other like a sick kitten leaning against a hot brick. They called to each other like mating seals.

Now their marriage has degenerated into a bogus buddy-hood. There is no more thrill at the sight of each other, no more "large charge in the main vein."

The wife's reaction is often unspiritual and singularly pathetic. The girl who was once the college beauty queen now stands on varicose veined legs and weeps into her dishwater. Her whole life has been seeing that the baby gets his bottle and that daddy doesn't get his.

She compensates for this by occasional dress-ups and buying sprees. She goes to one of her many club meetings dressed like Mrs. Astor's pet horse in order to find a little mercifully crisp conversation. She becomes a club addict and when she dies they could well inscribe on her tombstone: "Here lies Jane Smith—she was clubbed to death."

And the children . . . the little people at the other end of the telephone, to whom you say daily, "I'm sorry we can't get together, son, but you know how things are. Got to get the bread and butter, you know."

No wonder these precious kids clamor for attention by weird words, stupid antics, and odd ideas.

And their speech! As someone recently said, "Teenagers should be taught a second language—preferably English."

These heartbroken young frustrates are truly America's lonely people, who stand aghast at adult uncomprehension of their situation.

O, God knows, a nation can bear just so much unspiritual, materialistic secularizing before it crumbles.

Our nation is overclotted with this in our vital arteries and the church's greatest sin will be to ignore it.

What I have attempted to do is give you some vague pictures of the depth frustration involved in the analysis of the American home.

This has not been a brilliant or astute evaluation of the whole problem; but, under God, I level the challenge at my fellow frustrates in the seemingly impossible task of serving in the Lord's vineyard to accept the dedication of Joshua, another of God's men in a troubled time:

"As for me . . . and my house . . .

　　　　　　　. . . we will serve the Lord."

CHAPTER 6

How To Have A
Happy Hurricane

Hurricane Alma was a flirt.

She made eyes at Miami, mesmerized Palm Beach, and walked away with Fort Myers.

We all thought she would go out with Palm Beach, so we were dressing for the date.

Of course, we had to call our old standbys and cancel the evening with them.

As is often the case with a coquette, she stood us up.

At the time we thought we were The-Only-One-In-the-World-For-Her, we locked ourselves in and had a Hurricane Party.

This is a game Floridians play while the rest of the world thinks we're Dying Like Flies.

At our house, Pat strums his guitar, Mother frets, Dad writes sermons like this one, and Martha plays with our cat, Ali Baba (and his forty fleas!).

My secretary, Jackie Simpson, called our house to report

her safe arrival at her house, and finished the conversation with a cheery, "Bye—have a happy hurricane!"

The thought struck me that Christians have been having a happy hurricane for sixty-seven generations.

They have sat out many of them.

Mark's Gospel tells about one of the many hurricane parties experienced by the followers of Jesus.

The Lord was as much God as if He were not man at all . . .

. . . but He was also as much man as if He were not God at all.

As such, He was bushed—dog tired—after preaching from the prow of a boat at seaside to a throng on the shore. He was in the boat for possibly two reasons: the crowd would crush Him if He preached on shore and His voice carried better over water.

It was important to Him that He be heard.

But now He was tired, so He urged His disciples to get in the boat with Him.

Here's where you and I come into this sermon entitled, "How to Have a Happy Hurricane." If we are to ride out the storm, *we must make sure we get into the right boat* . . . an Unsinkable Molly Brown . . . and the one that has Jesus for the Captain.

Someone has said that an expert is a man who avoids small errors on the road to the Grand Blunder. The Grand Blunder for these disciples would have been to board some of the other little ships bobbling by the boat in which Jesus was resting.

I'll resist the temptation to spiritualize on what are some of the ships that never come in. I'll avoid that luxury but be assured that it is possible to get in the wrong boat.

The boat has always been the symbol of salvation. To get in the wrong boat simply means you have missed The Boat. There are boats and The Boat. There are ways and The Way. There are facts and The Truth. There is existence and The Life.

It does make a difference who captains your frail craft. It's a pretty good idea to be a bit choosy when it comes to selecting the vessel you intend to carry you over to the Other Shore.

After the disciples clambered on board, Jesus fell asleep in the boat. He had made Himself a little leather pillow, put His head upon it, and was sleeping the Sweet Sleep of a Quiet Conscience. He knew He could sleep well because His heavenly Father was wide awake.

The ship began to rock. As the waves began to threaten the little boat, the disciples made a terrific mistake—they set their nervous systems to the rhythm of the tossing boat rather than the quiet movement of the sleeping Saviour's bosom.

I'd rather be in a rocking boat with a calm Jesus than to be in a calm boat with a shaky captain. I've had to learn the joy of trusting Christ in the midst of chaos. Being a fellow pilgrim who knows the language of insomnia and the blues—I'm a semi-qualified companion in tribulation. Many nights I have counted more sheep than America owes dollars. Those nights have been equally divided. During the p.m. I thought I would die; during the a.m. I thought I wouldn't. What tunes the devil can play on tense, too tightly drawn nerves! The title of the song is, "The Rhythm of the Ruminator."

Our age is starved by the poverty of speed and saturation. A century ago, Ruskin was deeply shaken by the foregleams of this Age of Hurry. He could not be consoled "for the destitution of a London suburb by the softness of my own armchair."

He wrote, "No changing of pace at a hundred miles an hour, nor making of stuffs a thousand yards a minute, will make us one whit stronger, happier, or wiser. There was always more in the world than men could see, walked they ever so slowly; they will see it no better for going fast . . . As for being able to talk from place to place, that is indeed well and convenient; but suppose you have originally nothing to say? We shall be obliged at last to confess what we should long ago have known, that the really precious things are thought and sight, not pace. It does a bullet no good to go fast; and a man, if he truly be a man, no harm to go slow; for his glory is not all in going but in being."

Our age is hurrying—but with what . . . and to where? It would take a month of blue thunderstorms to list that catalogue of horrors man laughingly calls progress. Man is running for the Golden It and has an intense desire to lead the pack, but he has the gnawing fear that his deodorant has failed.

I sometimes think the reason man wants to move so swiftly is that he wants to become invisible, like Ruskin's bullet. If man is moving swiftly enough, he can't be stopped to philosophize about sin, sorrow, and death. You can't have a quiet talk with a passing bullet.

Have you ever noticed that when you are completely relaxed, the pace of your breathing is the same as that of the quiet waves that come into the shore? God can't speak to bullets but he can talk to completely composed Christians who sleep on leather pillows in the prow of the boat. Find God's rhythm and you won't worry about storms at sea.

John Haggai, the evangelist, says he is sure that when the Apostle Paul put his head on the chopping block . . . "his pulse was seventy-two."

You can have a happy hurricane but *you must make sure your boat is in the water.* Make sure Jesus is in the boat and that the boat is in the water. This is how you get to where you want to go. Some people got in the boat with Jesus but forgot to say, "Shove off."

Mind you, this is very safe. If you don't start the trip, you will never get in the storm. If you claim to be a Christian and there are no storms, it is due to the fact that you are not going anywhere.

A highborn Child of Royalty is made for direction and purpose. Perry Tanksley, a fine minister-poet, wrote:

> God grants a restlessness
> To birds in winterlands
> To flee through pathless skies,
> And guides them with His hand.
> God grants a restlessness
> To men who should respond,
> And some on wings of faith
> Fly toward their home beyond.
> For men, like helpless birds
> Are called to face the strife
> Birds find the sunny south,
> Men find eternal life.

No takeoff . . . no flight; no shove off . . . no sailing; no involvement . . . no Christian growth. God was able to send one Son to earth without sin; but never one without suffering. Involvement means suffering.

The fact that you are in a storm is proof that your boat is going somewhere. The trouble with too many Christians is that they wait until the storm is over before launching out. As John Russell, Chaplain at MIT says, "We look to the church to lead and often find it a reluctant caboose to the train of history." We've conveniently concerned ourselves with matters only obliquely related to the hot lava of human understanding.

While millions are fighting for the right to breathe free, we debate modes of worship, to see if we can't make it still a little more effeminate. Bishop Gerald Kennedy said it correctly, "The church with the most beautiful liturgy is probably the Russian Orthodox, yet they sat by while communism took over their country."

Real Christian love is not frightened at the prospect of battle—it seeks not limits but channels. In fact, real love hankers for a fight—it wants to knock some holy heaven into people. It bullies the devil. As Bud Robinson used to say, "The devil doesn't like this crowd . . . but it's mutual. We don't like him either. Anyway, we know more bad things on him than he knows on us."

Too many people want their church to be a quiet comfortable operation, where nobody gets hurt and nobody gets healed. If the Christians continue evading the Big Issues they will become a fading favorite, where men will no longer give their energy to us, considering it a bad investment. So shout . . .

. . . "Shove off!" The waters will be deep, chilly, and rough. But don't forget about the Man Asleep in the Prow of the Boat.

You can have a happy hurricane *if you make sure the water is not in the boat*. It is all right for the boat to be in the water but it is a Bad Day if the water is in the boat. This senile metaphor is good for one more round. It is all right for the church to be in the world but it is a Very Bad Day if the world is in the church.

The modern church can parade a galaxy of gimmicks. We use these to pump up the tire but we never patch the leak. This is why most pastors serve a congregation of Neurotics Unanimous who walk down the psychopath, live in the psycottage, and need to rest in the shade of the old psychiatry.

The modern church is not a throng of cackling phonies but neither is it a Museum of the True Blue. It is supposed to be an army—not a Hot House of Very Perishables. We must somehow learn to sing "Rescue the Perishables."

This is exactly our problem. We're too busy burping our billious backsliders not realizing there is an army of Goliaths just around the mountain.

. . . and here we are up Compromise Creek without a slingshot.

I'm always trying to blame somebody else for the church's sickness like the little brother who spread the jam on the baby's face so the finger of suspicion wouldn't be pointed at him. May the dear Lord teach me that the more candles on my birthday cake, the more like Jesus I am supposed to become.

As Willis Waldo, 80, told me recently, "I'm maturing."

And Kirk Harrell, 12, confided that Jimmy Sewell, 5, was maturing. "You see, pastor," he said, "Jimmy doesn't kick as often or pinch as hard."

God help us all to grow up but not in. Teach us to crucify worldliness, materialism, and compromise on the cross of commitment.

May we be like those early frustrated nobodies who disturbed our resting Lord with their frantic cries for salvation from the storm . . .

   . . . and heard Him shout, "Be muzzled."

   . . . and the waves ceased their growling.

CHAPTER 7

Get Tough, Protestants

One cannot say that a mainspring alone is a watch, but one can say that a watch would not be a watch without a mainspring.

One cannot say that Protestant Christianity alone made America, but one can say that America would not be America without it.

The best way to keep the Christian mainspring wound tightly is to treasure our golden moments.

To think of the hours when the battle was blackest, the crisis at its most exquisite redness, the crucible of pain at the moment of gore—and somebody stood tall.

It is my purpose in this uniquely important hour to write of those tall silhouettes, to draw renewed vigor, to encourage the timid breast to new dedication and action.

Among the ministers are the finest examples of royal manhood to be found, in a host of missionary Careys, freedom-loving Lelands, and some persecuted John Bunyans . . .

. . . all dry timber, simply waiting for the coming of the Great Fire.

I cannot accept that often-stated cliché, "There are no giants in the land anymore."

I believe there are so many giants standing together that they appear the same height—thus the illusion that we are giantless . . .

. . . and together we can move mountains if each one will carry his share of small stones.

You dare not be indifferent thinking your voice is unimportant. Remember, no drop of water feels responsible for a tidal wave.

You may feel you are but a moth hurling yourself into the incandescent brilliance of a massive smoldering revolution.

There is no cumulative effect which is not the sum total of an infinite number of parts.

If you remain spineless and voiceless, the total is one part less.

In the Grim Struggle before us we will not secure the freedom of men if we are less than the total of all parts functioning well—and together.

The massive concern of my heart is that our highborn, wellborn denominations are getting older. We dare not wait until we are too old to conceive to give birth to the Grand Cause that will continue the revolution born in the 1700s.

A denomination cannot wait until she is senile before becoming pregnant—it's too hard on the arthritis.

Old denominations, having evolved from the pentecostal to the mechanistic, never lead a crusade. Have you noticed? They always wait to see which course is "wise and prudent."

That is why they never die; they just fade away.

And the surest sign of denominational hardening of the "ardor"-ies is that they begin seeking another tired old church "grand and venerable" to lean on.

Then the two elderlies find another . . . and another . . . . . . and another.

Finally, you have a sort of retirement center for super-annuated, drowsy, non-relevant denominations.

I believe the word they use to cover up this blight . . . . . . is ecumenicity.

Before Protestantism decides to file for its Social Security check, perhaps it would be judicious to have a conference with our history.

Any action we take must be made as a covenant with our history and a pledge to our yet unborn.

Matters of infinite moment issue from simple beginnings.

It cost only seven thousand dollars to finance Columbus' discovery of America.

Dwight L. Moody said, "Every great movement can be traced to one kneeling figure."

I see Hubmaier on his knees facing the burning at the stake for believing the preachments of his inner soul . . .

. . . and Helwys and Smyth persecuted for the right of minority opinion.

. . . and John Bunyan, the shadow of prison bars across his face for thirteen years because he believed that discussion of public issues should be robust, uninhibited, and wide open.

. . . or Vavasor Powell, dying in prison, because of his conviction that all men should be free to believe or not believe.

See Roger Williams, kneeling in the snow, asking Providence to lead him to Providence, the fountain of waters, so he could find a place where every man is free to believe and practice what his conscience tells him.

This was ninety years before Thomas Jefferson was born, one hundred and fifty years before the Constitution was ever penned.

There had never been in the history of man a government granting absolute separation of church and state, recognizing religious liberty for all . . .

. . . let it be here recorded and heralded from this place throughout the world:

The first completely free government in the history of the world was founded and maintained by Protestants at Providence.

. . . see deeply convicted William Carey, struggling against the intolerant climate of hyper-Calvinism, laboring to convince a selfish age of the moral responsibility to proclaim liberty to the masses of faceless men, enshackled by heathenism. He later translated the Scriptures into the language of one-third of the population of the world.

Let it be recorded and heralded from this place throughout the world:

The power of the modern missionary movement was generated by Protestants.

. . . See Isaack Backus speaking before the framers of the Constitution who made up a skeptical audience because they could not foresee the repudiation of the established church.

Backus rode on horseback from house to house for the cause of religious liberty, preaching the inherent freedom of all men by creation and through the priesthood of all believers.

. . . See John Leland, the friend of Thomas Jefferson, James Madison, and George Washington, conversing with

Madison about the clamoring need for separation of church
and state to be a part of the Constitution of the United
States.

Let it be recorded and heralded from this place throughout the world:

The religion portion of the First Amendment to the Constitution of the United States is predominantly a Protestant
contribution.

. . . See Adoniram and Ann Hasseltine Judson, letting
their convictions be molded by what the Bible said rather
than what a council of tradition-ridden men said the Bible
said, who became missionaries and sent . . .

. . . Luther Rice to plead with churches in America,
ultimately forming the Triennial Convention in Philadelphia
in 1814.

The roll call of the outstanding can be listed ad infinitum,
ad boredom. But we get the drift of what they had in mind
and learn some potent lessons from them.

If John Wesley or George Whitefield had the subject,
"Great Moments in Protestant History," they would exclaim,
"Start exercising, the greatest moment in Christian history
is now."

We must never lose sight of the fact that the contem-
porary "now" is the time for greatness.

As Sam Humphries, chairman of our board in West Palm
Beach, says, "These great saints of the past were not history
watchers—they were history makers."

He's dead right about that.

We dare not let the future cave in on us while we look to
the past. Leave it to the historians to get the past straight,
let us dedicate ourselves to give the future a sure road.

If we feel resentment because of national trends, let us

sublimate our indignation into hard-nosed dedication and disciplined action . . .

. . . at it! at it! ever at it!

We can glory in the freedom of speech. But we have already lost it if we have nothing to say.

Which leads me to ask a serious question. What is the difference between the United States and the Soviet Union? There, they do not speak out because they are not allowed to. Here, we often do not speak out because we are afraid to.

In either case, nobody speaks.

What good is freedom of speech if we don't have nerve enough to say anything?

Bernard of Chartres in the twelfth century spoke of the value of history: We are "like dwarfs seated upon the shoulders of giants; we see more things than the ancients and things more distant, but this is due neither to the sharpness of our sight, nor the greatness of our minds, but because we are raised and born aloft on that giant mass."

If "we see more things than the ancients and things more distant . . ."

. . . and say less, what dwarfs we are!

If we see more, let us say more.

Edward Grey said fifty years ago that the United States is like "a gigantic boiler; there is no limit to the power it can generate."

The biggest question of our time is who will strike what match?

The Christian fire of freedom can ignite it—if enough of us become inflammable . . .

. . . if we repudiate the asbestine, fear-filled negativists who are so concerned about "the Protestant image."

When the church worries about its image, ignores surging

sociological upheavals, and becomes the Little Sir Echo of "me-too-ism," it is about as valuable as a tonsil.

We are the age that has discovered we are a sick generation; but the cost of moral reform is too high—so we economize by instructing the doctor to touch up the x-rays.

That we are a sick generation is not difficult to determine.

Someone called our time an elephant hanging from a cliff with its tail tied to a daisy.

This is due to the fact that in our play, God has not been given a speaking part. And all of this taking place when history's epileptic time clock seems about to run down.

When the masses need to be snatched from apathy we speak to them in clotted English with too many words chasing too little meaning.

Just when throngs are hanging by a neurotic emotional thread, we give everybody a pair of scissors.

To add to this delightful prospect, we come forth pleasantly unclear in our theology and unpleasantly clear in our immorality.

The day wallows deliciously in its prodigal swine-slime as the highest salary in the history of man is paid Elizabeth Taylor for doing Cleopatra—and I do mean doing.

Our *playwrights* are playwrongs whose ideas were belched from a Bronx sewer.

Our *movies* are a witch's brew, stirred in the cauldron of human agony to lure the Long Green, in a neurotic jealousy of television like the little boy who tells the nastiest story to gain attention.

Our *press* is no longer a symbol of the juggernaut for justice with the editorial page a prophet's pulpit. It is too often printed prevarication, too much toasted tripe, puffing exaggeration and eccentricity.

Print lice and license bring the stewardship of a free press into serious question.

The giants of journalism have become printing pygmies.

The fear of their poisoned arrows has caused us to be so frozen in our tracks that we have adopted as our slogan, "Don't just do something, stand there!"

Our *secular musicians* seem to have found the lost chord —and lost the rest of it. In the old days the music went round and round and the singers stood still. Now the singers go round and round and the music stands still . . . all flats with nobody sharp.

When I see some singers on TV, I realize there is an almost endless supply of village idiots.

We have reversed ancient Greece with its first-rate men and second-rate gods. We have a first-rate God and second-rate men.

A marriage of the best of ancient Greece and modern America would produce a spiritual conflagration that would leave the communist threat as a charred memory, an historic hangover.

O, we need great men in the ministry. Men who are mature enough to stand up under the pressures of modern churchmanship.

A church's vigor and tenacity in finding things for a preacher to do are enough to debilitate the United States Marine Corps. The program of a church can press down on you like the lid on a garbage pail.

We need preachers who can take it and can dish it out— not be one of those wavy-haired, horn-rimmed owls who wouldn't dream of giving a jolting glimpse of human frailty, who is the lead pilot in the yawn patrol.

I can't stand those inoffensive ninnies who have no ability

to relate themselves to an honest-to-satan person with a high imp quotient.

We do not need high-blown Hamlets. They will never convert this cynical world because they turn Biblical interpretation into watered stock.

I don't believe in slaughtering sacred cows but I love to try to milk them for the pure heaven of it.

We need men in the ministry, not the leaky, self-expressive drip—the kind that leaves a brown stain in the kitchen sink.

Listen to the words that were almost A. W. Tozer's last: "If the church of the second half of this century is to recover from the injuries she suffered in the first half, there must be a new type preacher. The old prophet type who stands in flat contradiction to everything our smirking smooth civilization holds dear."

We need the kind who can tell the difference between people who possess real character and those who merely flash credentials. The sort of minister who is the chief executioner of people who take themselves seriously and the Lord not seriously at all.

The old-time preacher may not have been given a new car by the church as a reward for not offending anybody, but he got around the membership well enough to produce a generation of high-calibered people who knew what sin and grace were.

Charles Spurgeon generally stayed up to his baptistry boots in holy hot water for thundering righteousness to a wide-awake congregation.

The old-time preacher didn't have that neurotic fixation upon being loved by just everybody or "I'll die."

He might not have been the most popular man in town

and that bothered him so much he couldn't go to sleep until just after dark!

He wasn't the most sought after banquet speaker and invocationist, but no one ever made fun of him the way journalists do of modern men of the cloth.

John Bunyan was as poor as a gopher but he kept on digging until he struck gold in human need by writing *Pilgrim's Progress.*

Not much great preaching sprouts in subsidized soil.

Walter Rauschenbusch could have related the Gospel to those beatniks who go around mumbling, looking sick, don't wash, and scratch a lot. He would have told them that Jesus found his disciples from a scurvy group just like them—and he would have ripped the comic stuffing out of their detachment.

Another group he would have made fun of are the super pious "I am God's little brother" group. You know who they are. They're the ones who want to label the rest rooms "Brothers" and "Sisters." These holy ones who think they have an exclusive hot line to Heaven, in reality, as Nancy James says, have an I.Q. just below plant life.

He would have brought them back to reality with a shock of ice water which came from his veins, since he went around looking for stuffed shirts to poke with his umbrella.

He was an ego-buster of saints and sinners who offered a take-it-or-leave-it attitude to God's frozen people, who stood silently before clamoring social upheavals.

The old-time preacher didn't hunt for sinners in a Ferrari built for two but he found them, gentlemen.

Do you?

And his churches had a way of staying together. He never preached that the church is a democracy. He always preached that it was a fellowship and anybody who broke the fellowship couldn't vote. His churches didn't pay any attention to the tantrum-prone.

My son Pat explained to me not long ago why the dirigible Hindenburg blew up and burned. The chambers were in too close proximity. That's just the reason churches explode also. Too many gas bags too close to each other.

A few friction sparks and the conflagration is well around us . . .

. . . and the odor therefrom is a stench in the nostrils of a holy Lord.

It is easy to point up the qualities of the men of the past but there is a danger here.

Because we had rather tell the story of the burning of Hubmaier and the slaying of Bill Wallace as material to enliven our sermons and build our congregations than to use their methods and lose our following.

Remember, not every layman who says he wants his minister to be a courageous man of God will put up with him if he becomes one.

Honestly now, how long has it been since you stood with an obvious minority for a principle you love.

It won't hurt us to journey down Freedom Walk and get some new spine.

I see an Obadiah Holmes whiplashed for the Gospel until his back "was like jelly" and I think of the modern cleric, deeply upset if he is disliked by only one member of his church.

I see Hubmaier cremated for Christ and I think of the greatest heretic of all history, the average American, mumbling an ignorant "It doesn't make any difference what you believe—so long as you are sincere."

This kind of abusing the brain God gave us has set Christianity back a thousand years.

American middle-class Protestantism is thoughtlessly advocating a cube-root-of-nothing syncretism of religion that strikes an average of several mediocre groups.

The result is a poor finish, far below the standards of the New Testament, which is the only standard God ever blessed.

I recognize the taboos put upon this kind of talk. Thomas Griffith aptly warns us not to walk into the "barracuda waters" if we don't expect to get chewed on.

But let's take on all this ecumenical talk and see if it makes any sense.

I am convinced that most denominations are hermetically sealed in the tin of uniformity and want no Christian minister to get a can opener.

Take ten buckets, each containing fifty per cent oil and fifty per cent water. Pour them into a large container. What do you have?

Fifty per cent oil and fifty per cent water.

Put several impotent denominations into one group.

What do you have?

You have solved the problem. You no longer have several small impotent denominations. You now have one large impotent denomination.

And there is less possibility of reformation within a giant institutional superdenomination than within the smaller units.

They still call that period of time when there was just One Church, the Dark Ages.

It does appear that we face a historical cyclical return to a deeper darkness than before.

Your grandson may be called upon to die for his convictions.

Mr. Christian, you'd better make up your mind to be Christian.

Because if you are unsure about your convictions, you will be jarred out of the saddle your first trip out.

Let us continue the Reformation!

Let us carry it to its logical conclusion!

Stand tall and walk right past the incense, the robes, the ritual, and the regulations into the free air of the open New Testament and show the world how free-born, happy Christians should live.

Let us show a haunted hungry world that we can put wholesome blood in its veins, not the embalming fluid of a giant ecumenical corpse.

Let us show that that Martyn Lloyd Jones was right when he said that putting all denominational corpses in one ecclesiastical graveyard will not make a resurrection. When the resurrection morning *does* come, they'll be the first up because the Bible says, "The dead in Christ shall rise first."

We dare not be denominational dullards and party-line bores.

We dare not average ourselves out because we will lose social status if we do.

Remember, the average is the worst of the best and the best of the worst.

Who wants to be that?

Not I!

Do you?

Let us separate from the Great Corpse. If we joined them they would respect us less.

If we united with them, they would have us in a relationship of regulation. I can hear them yell the first time we refused to cooperate:

"Spurgeon, Truett, Calvin, Knox,
Give it to the orthodox!"
We would be the bad egg in the ecumenical omelet.
Let us face it, gentlemen.
We do not want in and they do not want us in.
Why?

Because we would insist on the elimination of all tradition that has taken the place of the teachings of the Word of God.

Because we would insist on a paper pope called the Bible instead of a human one called Paul.

Because we would insist on the Lordship of Christ instead of the headship of a Church.

Because we would insist on separation of church and state and religious liberty for all men all over the world . . . and that just might offend some of the separated brethren.

Because we would remind the new Superdenomination that forty per cent of all wars fought since the seventh century have been related to the church-state merger. The United States of America has never been engaged in such a war. No other major nation on earth can make that statement.

The danger of church-state coalitions in any Siamese combination endangers both of the twins.

Perfectly blind to the obvious lessons of history, huge, normally respectable denominations go to the back door of the White House to ask for a handout. Some day the White House will feed them . . .

. . . then make them chop wood for their new Master. This is the modern version of the rail-splitter.

Benjamin Franklin knew this was coming. He said, "When a religion is good, I conceive that it will support itself and when it cannot support itself and God does not take care to support it, so that its professors are obligated to call for help of the civil power, it is a sign, I apprehend, of its being a bad one."

But how could Benjamin Franklin know anything? He had never heard of penicillin—or Disneyland.

I'll tell you, it did something to me when I heard that Glenn L. Archer was compelled to say of us: "Some hospital directors seem more interested in institutional security than in free worship for their children. There are college presidents who have been more concerned about a new building than they have been concerned about the values of true education."

I was shamed when I read that the brilliant Jewish constitutional lawyer, Leo Pfeffer, said, "I wonder if this is what it is coming to—that we dissenters are taking up the fight that you Baptists are getting ready to abandon."

And Mr. Archer jarred me when he said, "If we are too weak to fight and too fat to run, we shall have lost America's most precious heritage."

American Christians will be historically pertinent so long as they are made to appear radical when judged by European ecclesiastical institutions.

When we are "blended," they will become valueless . . . would it not be a tragedy indeed if Christians became apologetic just before the dawn of victory for freedom among the peoples of the earth?"

Protestants, with all that grand name implies, don't wring your hands; ring the Liberty Bell!

CHAPTER 8

How To Live With A Pharisee By Trying Real Hard

The chief prophet of the Sour Set is the pharisee.

He exchanges a birthright for a mess of pottage.

Everything he touches turns to gall.

Like Sunday, for instance.

A dog doesn't dare scratch a flea on this holy day lest he be indicted for Sabbath desecration. It seems that every flower stops blooming at midnight of the pharisee's Sunday. The rooster rests his little larynx . . .

. . . even Alka Seltzer refuses to work.

Nobody ever received a spiritual blessing while bored. The severe Sabbath of stringency is the spoilsport of happy Christianity.

Like attitude, for instance.

When he speaks of Christian love, his tones are like oleaginous butter. When he speaks of other people's sins, his talk is nine parts drool.

What he hasn't learned, as Cort Flint says, is that the

Holy Spirit will not waste his time revealing to a person another man's sins.

To him, the world tastes of indigestible sourness, the dark brown taste in the roof of his psyche.

To detect some virile sinner in a relatively mild violation of one of The Rules stirs volumes of venom within him.

Some of The Rules are man-made and typical of Jesus' description of how the pharisaic mind uses tradition to super-cede Scripture (Matthew 15:1f; 16:1f).

He feels he has the right to supplant or twist the Scripture because he role-plays as god-the-judge all the time.

This mind pattern will be proclaimed a little tin god or he'll blow up the church.

Personal ego is his Rome and every utterance is *ex cathedra*. His only close friend is a mirror, before which he prays "Our Father. . . ."

His judgmental attitude eliminates understanding love. To divulge your deepest secret to him is the equivalent of having close communion with a hydrogen bomb. He is president of the Royal Order of Back Stabbers.

He oozes ossified orthodoxies and is the patron saint of schism.

This Religious Rule Setter will tie a knot around your once happy heart that will make the Gordian seem as loose as an arthritic's bowstring.

Like volume, for instance.

He blows his horn and yells but when no wall of anybody's Jericho comes crashing down, his response is an increase of decibels instead of sober reflection.

Those who have to live with him, long for the quiet Fun of the Highborn. No such pleasure comes because joy and he are antonyms.

He delights to ugly up the happy.

With paranoia at the throttle, his irresistible energy continually searches for some calm center to stir up . . . and he does it in the name of God.

This disturber of Christian composure spreads the virus of petty meddling, always dropping atomic bombs on mocking birds—much blow over nothing.

This much ado about zeroes covers up his lack of compassion and diverts attention from the fact.

Jesus went about seeking to cosign notes with the morally bankrupt. These are they who cannot help themselves and will never find the Happy Way unless someone steps up in their behalf.

The pharisee looks for the appropriate moment—that is when other religious professionals are looking away—and steps on the heads of the helpless.

If there are degrees in hell, he'll get the hot spot on the rotisserie of eternity's oven.

As Alexander Pope said, "The worst of madmen is a saint gone mad."

His favorite verse is "now abideth faith, hope, and charity; and the greatest of these is criticism."

Every time true Christianity plants a moral root that will result in the fruit of redemption, he enters into a real, righteous, reformation campaign and plows up all the good already done.

One has the feeling that H.J. (Holy Joe) does not really want sinners to repent, like the elder brother in the story of the prodigal son. While the happy father was killing the fatted calf, putting the ring of sonship on the returnee's finger, and draping the robe of acceptance upon his back, the elder brother pouted and fumed in jealousy.

The flip-side application of Jesus' point in the story:
"There is rejoicing in heaven over one sinner who repents"
is that there should be equal rejoicing on earth because one
of the Lord's wayward children has staggered home.

This sanctified scab cannot rejoice when an obvious sinner
repents because he has used such a person as the backdrop
to highlight the contrast of his own self-righteousness.

Pharisees need for wicked sinners to remain vile. The
sinner is someone to point at. When H. J. points, he points
away from himself, thus diverting attention from his own
imperfections and increasing the contrast between himself
and the prodigal.

Jesus prayed "Thy will be done in earth as it is in heaven."
He meant for us to react on earth as heaven reacts.

If this be true, the church should go into an absolute colic
of hilarity when one sinner comes home.

One of the keys to redeeming a self-righteous person is to
take away his cause for boasting of his home-wrought goodness.

Isn't this the point of the story of the pharisee and the
publican? In this case H. J. was the president of the Royal
Order of Breast-Beaters. Listen to him bray, "I thank thee
that I am not as other men are. . . ."

So are we.

" . . . even as this publican."

See how he uses this other person as an illustration of his
personal goodness.

Jesus saw through all this—He always does—and said H.J.
was one of those "who trusted in themselves that they were
righteous and despised others" (Luke 18:9).

The only way to live with such a person is to be intolerant
of his intolerance.

As Gert Behanna says, "I am a snob. I look down on people who look down on people."

If you resist him in this fashion you can expect him to come at you like a bull elephant with a mad on.

He'll speak to you and of you like eight thunderstorms but you must keep up the pressure because it is the only way to break his precast psychic mind-set.

His rhino charge will come at you with bullying fascism. There is no fence limiting the lies he will tell to bring you down.

As Paul says, he will "spy out your liberty" and do everything in his power to enchain you and break your spirit. You simply must not let him overwhelm you. Everytime he slaps you, hit him in return with a great big dose of love. If you keep it up he will either repent or crucify you.

In what ways will he try to crucify you?

He will demand that you give patent, simple answers to life's complex problems. He has a growing thirst for drastic solutions.

When you honestly cannot give an uncomplicated answer because no such answer exists, he then will damn you publicly and give a two plus two formula—which the public wants to buy but will never try.

He thus emerges on the white horse and you are the man in the black hat—hissed and booed off the platform.

The secret of his power is that he gives the mindless segment of the public an easy road to expiate their guilt and express their vital virility. He leads them into a crusade which he fronts until it begins to sputter. It is then that he seeks a scapegoat leader and bows out, blending himself into the crowd.

By the time the populus wakens to discover that the

nightmare is actually gooed-up reality, the pharisee is out in the crowd sowing seeds of discord and dissention and giving voice lessons on how to say "crucify him."

It is at this point that H.J. quietly gurgles that, while he would never seek the position himself, if the people demand his return—much as he would prefer that some good brother have the opportunity to serve—he will humbly offer himself as a sacrificial lamb.

He then can do no wrong. They *forced* him into leadership.

Until his dying day he will seek the maintenance of his status posture no matter what the cost to the group he serves.

When he goes through such prostitution of public or group trust, your job is to keep your head and don't pucker. Keep tight-lipped and pray.

The fascism of the pharisee causes him, like the skunk, to pollute the atmosphere. It is almost impossible to breathe there.

Just hold your nose and plow straight into him. This is exactly what Jesus did. The only people with whom he was harsh were the pharisees who had all the answers.

The Lord refused to allow their oversimplification of issues.

So must you.

The Lord refused to be frightened into neutrality by their ingenius use of invective.

So must you.

The Lord stood up to them when they questioned his motives and loyalties.

So must you.

Almost the whole world is afraid to say what it believes for fear of getting into trouble that results in character assassination and all kinds of unpleasantness and embarrassment.

The Lord called them "fools, blind guides, hypocrites."

You must do the same.

This is get-tough-protestantism sure enough.

Their response to this will be the cry that you are a disturber of Christian unity. They hold an unbelievably naive concept of fellowship; which, upon close examination, reveals itself to be a mindless and unquestioning obedience to a religion that is Victorian and very applicable to the latter part of the nineteenth century. This is the paranoid style of the modern church.

They have so neutralized free discussions that it is necessary they be equally paralyzed so discussion can be free and equal.

But watch their Machiavellian method. Any discussion on their part will be to ventilate feelings rather than generate light and life. They seem more interested in winning arguments than influencing destiny.

We can never make theology again the queen of the sciences and the church the most influential community of men in the world until the mass hysteria of irrational debate and political deceit be stopped.

Whole segments of several denominations are dominated by this sort of thought control. What happens to the average member of these communions is important. The vital-minded pastor is one of the keys to the spiritual destiny of the people of God. Yet the minister can not realize his spiritual powers as long as he cowers before neurotic bureaucracy.

The people must believe in the fact that the pastor is a Christ-possessed man. They must be able to say, "Here is a man who thinks for himself."

He must never consider if his plan is all right with everybody, especially the acknowledged members of the denominational Sanhedrin.

The answers to any community need is best known by its residents. Those Christians who prate their belief in the priesthood of all believers must also believe in the priesthood of each community.

Pharisaism at the top corrupts all the way down, resulting in an increase of righteous rhetoric. If there is anything the church doesn't need it is more words.

The only way the world will be changed is to balance deed with preachment. With each pulpit decibel increase there must be a matching love-deed-for-Christ done in the community.

CHAPTER 9

The Ecumenicity Of
Red Blood

I am a clergyman.

It is my responsibility to try to guide the four thousand souls who are members of my congregation.

When, a few years ago, I became their minister, I found myself thrilled at the prospect of serving so large a congregation. It had all the ego factors a semi-secularized, materialistically-minded minister could want.

It was a great church that could be greater—in terms of physical and numerical growth.

The record was *bound* to look good . . .

. . . and now, nearly six years later, the record does just that. In fact, the church has achieved some little national recognition. Articles have been written about it, committees come to investigate our program, different denominations use our plan as recommended procedure; and a motion picture has been produced using this minister and his church as the subject.

The church has been mentioned in several books.

I have been asked to speak on national convention platforms, ministers' conferences, even executive motivational meetings.

At forty-one years of age I have everything a person could want—an almost adequate salary, a beautiful parsonage, a magnificent church, a loving wife and two very normal children.

The whole thing is Great Big.

But lately . . .

. . . in the middle of the night . . .

. . . I've begun to miss something.

When I was a very young minister I felt something I wish I could feel again.

I heard something I wish I could hear again.

It was the sound of Sandaled Feet walking beside me.

Now I have convention buttons; doctors degrees; plaques; photographs of me with movie stars, a president, and other dignitaries; fund-raising awards, and dozens of other gewgaws and gadgets.

But I find myself wanting more than anything else . . .

. . . to hear again those Quiet Steps . . .

of the Sandaled Feet.

I discover myself wanting an old-fashioned baptism of Realism.

I have motivated thousands of people to one degree or another.

But how many have I touched with *The Touch?*

When the smoke clears away, this is the only question that counts.

Let me naively trust the basic goodness and good will of all who read this and let my pen flow as the Spirit directs.

To begin with, I am a denominationalist.

The ecumenical movement has always seemed to be too vast, too political, and based on too broad principles to be effective.

My denomination has not united in the effort for what those of us who study it consider good reasons.

Some have said we have been too smug, too inbred on this point.

And to some degree, they are right.

I must admit that there are those among us who feel that the Spirit of God cannot or does not work outside the framework of Our Four Walls.

Most of us do not believe this, to be sure; but we have had to bear the bad image of those few who do.

A minister must be faced with a choice of working inside a denominational structure or out of it.

I have chosen to work in it but it must be admitted that there are problems in doing so.

A denomination must make up its mind as to whether it will be a radiant corporate fellowship or an ecclesiastical politicism. Actually, the Southern Baptists are both. Some among us are politically minded—to a terrifying degree. To threaten the power of denominational leadership incurs their violent wrath—with swift, mindless, and devastating attack upon the character and intentions of any young minister who aspires to be a potential leader.

This has happened so many times it has become a recognizable pattern.

The creative well-springs of many have been dried up because of fear of these politico-ecclesiastics.

Fortunately, this group represents an infinitesimally small segment of our larger fellowship.

One who is really sincere should never fear these pious pythons. Their paranoia gives them an exaggerated sense of power, which the Good Guys in our big family will never allow to dominate.

It is these Good Guys who make it worth while and offer such great hope for any church or denomination.

There is much in any denomination to love. The humility of the members of boards and agencies; the leaders who strive to find new ways of winning men to Christ; the hosts of pastors who only want to have a place to serve the Lord; the educators wrestling with the problem of quality education on short income; the religious editors who wait to hear both sides of the story before printing anything—the fair-minded, the honest, the humble, the Quiet Ones.

There is much—very much—in such a fellowship to love.

A denomination will be great so long as its leaders can still hear the sound of the Sandaled Feet.

A leader can be humble and avoid being a threat to anyone else who also leads.

W. G. Watson, President of Crozer Theological Seminary —a leader himself—said at the funeral of Dwight L. Moody, "I'd rather be Dwight L. Moody dead, lying there in his coffin, than any living man on earth."

No jealousy between these giants!

These men moved the world because of the obvious conformity of their lives to the life of Jesus.

You could hear the quiet sound of Sandaled Feet walking in the hallways of their hearts.

I was talking about our isolation from the ecumenical movement. I said we stay out of it for very good reasons.

The thing that worries me is that though the reasons are good, they are complicated to explain and it takes time to sit down with each questioner and sophisticate a reply of any convincing value.

Now we don't have time to sit down with millions of people and explain the long rigamarole.

Therefore, millions of people think we are a Big Bunch of Prudes.

And, in too many instances, we are.

The impression many people get is that we are a Giant Vacuum of Wrongheadedness, a huge sect of oddness, a frenetic flutterbrain with a charley horse between our ears.

We protest that this isn't true.

They say, "Okay, explain it."

We say, "Have you got two hours?"

They say, "No."

We say, "Then, I can't explain it."

So we part.

And they think our solution to world problems is, "I've only got two hands and I'm busy wringing them."

Now, let me explain briefly—not my deepest thoughts—but my deepest emotions about churches.

Let's take the Roman Catholics, as an example.

I can remember when we thought of them as a Hooded Medievalism, shrouded in mystery, and a Threat to America.

I can recall Sunday-morning sermons on "The Catholic Menace." I have preached them.

There was a time when I was a boy that I wouldn't have been surprised if a little Catholic boy cut his foot on a nail, to see green blood—or some other odd color—come out. If he had been from Mars I would not have thought him to be more other—and odd.

But we saw a lot of Catholic blood in World War II, Korea, and Viet Nam . . . all of it was red, Just Like Ours.

So we became one, physically.

It is this sameness of humanity that is very important to emphasize.

So may it be clearly said that most of us believe in the Ecumenicity of Red Blood.

Anyone who doesn't simply hasn't joined the human race.

This great oneness should make each one of us be humble before the other.

Hear the parable of Two Old Goats.

They met on a ledge too narrow to pass. Neither would back down—Old Goats are like that. But if they butted horns they would fall hundreds of feet to their deaths.

So they stood there, glaring at the other for hours.

Finally, one Old Goat said, "Something must be done. We have a choice here—cooperate or die."

The other said, "I won't give in to you. I know you won't give in to me."

The first Old Goat reasoned, "If we each give in to the other at the same time, we can keep our identity and live on. I'll give in if you will."

So he knelt down low.

And the first Old Goat passed over the other . . .

. . . and both went on their way.

The Ecumenicity of Red Blood will make one Old Goat give in to another and both will be benefited.

This kind of ecumenicity will cause me to live in my world with such a sense of respect for all men that causes me to give in to my fellowman—making it easier for him to go down life's road.

It cannot be God's will that I make it more difficult for him.

There is nothing so lovable as an Old Goat who has repented.

Another thing the Ecumenicity of Red Blood will do is bring the laboratory of life back to an appreciation of man rather than the Deification of Machines.

The degree to which men are beginning to trust machines is frightening.

A writer famous in Hungary in the Thirties was Frigyes Karinthy. He writes that in Budapest the people thronged to a little restaurant where they could put a coin in a slot and food would come out of the machine. The truth was that a little man concealed himself inside the so-called machine. He would catch the money in his hand, then put the food through the door.

The little man was an early prophet who saw that man was beginning to trust machines more than people.

He was successful in direct proportion to his ability to put the image of a machine between him and the people.

Perhaps man trusts a machine more because man is becoming a machine without knowing it. Machines don't bleed Red Blood, cry, or psychically regurgitate, so man is jealous and wants to be machine-like because of the consistency and seeming maturity of a machine.

The cause of the deification of the machine is the worship of amoral science.

The Ecumenicity of Red Blood will give science a moral consciousness.

Arthur Miller made a speech before a congress of American psychologists in which he pointed out that without human values one doesn't even come up with a good science.

He illustrated his point by telling of research made by the Nazi doctors in which they made experiments with people by dropping them into a swimming pool, having connected instruments to their bodies to measure what hap-

pened when a man was drowning. Never had such measure-
ments been undertaken. Previously, only autopsies could
be made after the deaths of drowned persons.

Miller pointed out that this might cause an increase of
knowledge but it isn't science.

After his speech, Miller was deluged with criticisms from
about twenty-five of the professional psychologists.

"Why isn't it scientifc?" they demanded.

Mind you, this was not Dachau but New York City.

This immoral attitude is the cause of the sterility of the
Womb that gives birth to ministers, philosophers, poets,
and other interpreters of the human spirit. The result will be
that we have much ability but nothing to say—much thrust
but no direction.

An orbitless comet is extremely dangerous.

We are seeing illustrations of this all around us.

It was my privilege to introduce Colonel John Glenn to
the pastors of our denomination, more than eight thousand
of them.

In his speech he repudiated what I call *Astrodopes*, that
is, those who emphasize Time and Space with no reference
to Theos and Spirituality.

On the other side of the coin there are the *Theodopes*,
those who worship a God-Out-There with no reference to
things as they are here and now.

What we need is a happy marriage between the *Astrodopes* and the *Theodopes*. Perhaps someday we will pro-
nounce them husband and wife—*Theostros*— Science and
Faith.

And to our Heavenly Father of the bride, we say, "Best
wishes, You haven't lost a daughter—You have gained a
laboratory!"

May our time measure men, not by Freud, Jung, or the Behaviorists—but by Jesus Christ who gave the measure of what men ought to be.

If we admit that the rules were set by Freud or Jung, we admit that our research only goes back to 1912.

Let us take it back at least two thousand years.

CHAPTER 10

Foolfathers

Tomorrow's children will be born if radiation allows it.

If, by atomic stupidity, they happen to have three ears, I hope we have one or two solid facts to say into at least one of them.

Our generation, foolishly basking in the warming rays of the reflection of the hydrogen blast, has been profligately spending two reservoirs of wealth: yesterday's heritage and tomorrow's money.

When we have wasted away both of these priceless possessions and our yet unborn stand nude and spiritually poor, they will orate, "Our foolfathers (that's what they will call us) handed us a burned-out torch and told us to run with it . . .

. . . "and we are running—but we know not why or where.

"They bathed us with theological liberalism, denominational syncretism, philosophical relativism, and ministerial mush.

"While singing 'How Firm a Foundation' they rejected the Chief Cornerstone, and built on religious jello."

Thus will intone the chorus of the future . . .

. . . unless

. . . unless what?

. . . unless we realize that presently we have been living on the impetus, the force, the drive of a godly ancestry. When that force is spent, we will really understand the meaning of poverty . . .

. . . unless we concretize some convictions that will actively go to war against liberal looseness and fundamental lovelessness.

. . . unless the simple Christ life becomes the norm or illumination that will guide us down the presently darkened path of foggy blah with few streetlights, the unknowns seeming more unknowable with each passing hiccup of history's intoxicated clock.

We have become, as Earl Nightingale says, a nation of followers following followers who are following followers.

Like the foreman who set his watch by the clock in the jewelry store window. He did this every morning for ten years. One day the jeweler said, "Joe, what do you do at the factory?"

"I blow the factory whistle at noon and quitting time."

"That's interesting," said Jake, the jeweler. "For ten years I've been setting this clock by that whistle."

There we are!

The dog chasing his own tail—and calling it progress.

As a dumb blonde I know said, with wisdom clothed in stupid garments: "Gollie, it looks like we are progressing into obscurity."

Let us keep a tenacious grip on the iron will to turn the

helm of the listing craft of the family of man.

The modern minister, having given ten hours a day patching the sails in his listless ship, has little time or inclination to act like a prophet, and often preaches sermons that are monotonous monologues, in which events must be deciphered from the hieroglyphic language of the theologians.

O, when will we learn that, to the man on the street, the issue is not Bultman and Barth but babies and bills.

Let us reach in the stratosphere and pull the truth down to earth.

A minister is not an exurban hypochondriac whose sermons are a seance on a sunny Sunday morning.

A real preacher-prophet builds beams into men's dreams —if their dreams be built of gritty substance rather than oozing the acid of Ivy League cynicism.

He must not think prophecy is spunky debunking but compassionate, courageous swimming in the spiritual and sociological swells.

It is not the church's role to scowl and scold but to diagnose, prescribe, accept . . .

. . . and love like heaven!

Evangelism is this and nothing more.

There is nothing more inimical to human faith than an unsure minister. But the too sure man-of-the-cloth is also a threat. As one of them said one time, "Give me twenty minutes and I'll preach everything I know and several things I'm not sure of."

Laymen would breathe easier if their pastor ever admitted that he is not omniscient.

It isn't necessary that we be right on EVERY issue.

We can admit being human, subject to error, and yet be loved.

Not even to a pope is EVERY utterance ex cathedra.

Worse than being mistaken at times is the image that a perfectionistic personal vanity has become identified with men of God.

We must take the Gospel, not ourselves, seriously.

How dangerous it is to be completely serious about everything. There is no buffoonery more absurd than a man who is constantly attempting to imitate himself.

He will think he is a Big Wheel when in reality he is only going around in circles.

Bricks and self-worshipping ministers won't float for long.

The church cannot afford the luxury of seeming either as a bilious, tantrumy finger-wagger or a doting grandmother, tolerating everything.

I speak to the men who speak for the Lord's Church who should be saying with Paul, that wondrous apostle of Grace, "I am proud of the Gospel. It is God's saving power for everyone who believes . . . ." Romans 1:16 (Centenary Translation).

Christian dialogue is not a process of exchange where we cancel out each other's certitudes . . .

. . . it is a fellowship of passionate digging for truth.

We cannot find this if our ministers are hale-and-hollow clergymen who speak to each other through tightened lips with true fraternal venom.

Don't you feel a sense of spiritual griminess with our surface unity covering divisions and shenanigans?

We need ministers who will surrender themselves to prophethood.

We have been urged to try preaching doubts to see if we like it. This is like urging a man to try suicide to see if he learns anything from it.

Liberalism will cause a great awakening, we are told. We have observed that national religious revivals have always been led by Bible-believing conservatives. We have seen several major denominations try the way of the far left, theologically.

Where are they now?

Was there power as a result?

Were thousands converted?

Were new churches born?

The record is clear. Decay was augmented, churches were divided, ministers lost their evangelistic zeal, the common touch vanished, the denominations became snob hatcheries, and there was a gravitation to identify with the middle to upper classes of society only.

The claim that they offer new methods turns out to be some weak retreads. We need brand-new, puncture-proof tires to take us over the rocky paths ahead.

We live in a tired time when the only people with energy enough to go on are the hysterical . . .

Let us imitate our brothers who are called evangelists—who, like the first evangelist, the Apostle John, thought it not improper to give first place to heralding the Gospel.

Let us crucify thumb twiddling in a troubled time . . .

. . . and ecclesiastical clutter

. . . and denominational butter

. . . and rebellious mutter

. . . and rebellious mutter

. . . and the pastoral strutter

. . . and the Gospel stutter

. . . and preach to this psychically ill, sensate age the grandest news of all—that Jesus Christ has come!

O Witnesses of the Holy Word,

Make safe mediocrity appear ugly.

Give testimony with courage and sledge-hammer style.

Make our nice age sick with conviction.

Break the hearts of the true saints.

Expose the hypocrite without being one yourself.

Dig us up, but don't bury us.

Pour some spiritual optimism into our decadent day.

Frown on sin.

Forget the word, "Image," remembering only the image of Jesus.

Tell the ecclesiastical know-it-alls to go to heaven.

If we don't wake up now we'll slumber in the soft bed of irrelevancy forever.

You are royal sons of the King.

Act like it.

Prepare. Prepare. Prepare.

Shoot at us, shake us, then soothe us.

Don't let us revel in our own righteousness.

Pray with suction.

Find the filling of the Spirit.

Cry aloud.

Spare not.

Millions of broken-hearted frustrates need you.

While preaching about the building campaign, the attendance goals, the newest dance, the atom bomb, and the dangers of Rosecrucianism, it might be good to sprinkle in a little Gospel "just for old time's sake."

The modernists have sent no more people to hell than the adenoidal lungbusters who are as dogmatic as a kamikazi pilot.

To hear this sort of preaching is like listening to a thunder-clap in a phone booth.

Our age has grown tired and spiritually discouraged. Put us back in the march against time.

The sands are rapidly falling into the lower lobe . . .

There may not be too many grains left.

So get at it!

Beat the relativism out of us.

Cure us of poor-mouthing, pre-bottled pulpit pap of sophomoric slush.

Stop all this silly talk about the post-Protestant, post-Christian era.

The Gospel is not a faintly flickering fire, around which cowardly church members must huddle to keep the winds of Sartre from blowing it out.

Double up your incentive . . .

. . . and tell us to repent or prepare to die as other arrogant grand societies have done.

The church has been the pallbearer of many proud nations that predicted the death of the Gospel.

The church is now beginning to write the funeral sermon for this nation if it will not turn.

God forbid—but that sermon may have to be preached in the next 100 years.

. . . and we are to blame for it!

God is not dead but America may be.

We have imprisoned God in a box called the sanctuary.

We have adopted a wait-and-see-which-way-the-wind-blows ethic.

We have stood like a blind man in an art gallery before the liberating doctrines of our virile faith.

You can't quote, "God's in His heaven, all's right with the world."

When your congregation, no longer a blind herd, knows

good and well . . . that 11 per cent of the female students of a major university became pregnant in one year . . .

. . . that by 1970, according to the late and lamented Peter Howard, there will be ten million illegitimate children in the United States . . .

. . . that, according to TIME magazine (April 5, 1963, p. 94), 80 per cent of the whiskey of the world is drunk by Americans . . .

. . . that there are 500 cocktail parties a day in Washington, D.C. . . .

. . . that 75 per cent of college students cheat on exams —and admit it . . .

. . . that 51 per cent of the divorces in the world take place in the United States . . .

. . . that, according to Bob Alexander of Truth, Inc., in a business employing 270 employees, 227 admitted habitually stealing from the company.

. . . In the midst of these pleasant prospects, I ask you, my brothers in the ministry,

What do you offer the world?

One who pursues terminology instead of content?

A clotheshorse and a trained larynx?

An autocratic mind set?

One who coddles factious lay groups?

As an administrator, are you a stern taskmaster?

As a preacher, are you a compassionless moralist?

As a denominationalist, a party-line bore?

As a human being, a parochial bumpkin?

As a husband, a Caesar . . .

. . . and your wife a lady Jonah who thinks of you as Nineveh and longs for some decent whale to come along and swallow her up?

If so . . .

. . . you'll do about as much good for the world as an aspirin dispenser at a leper colony . . .

. . . and you'll end up resting in the shade of the old psychiatry.

None dare call it reason.

Or . . .

. . . you can be a courageous, compassionate, character-filled servant-minister, faithful to the Word of God . . .

. . . who can hear the trumpet call to duty at the dawning of every day.

O, be a glove into which the hand of God can fit.

CHAPTER 11

How To Kill A Denomination Without Really Trying

A denomination can degenerate until it becomes a sweating, groaning, grunting, wrestling match between the politicians of ambition and the pietists of ideals.

The fall of a denomination is always gradual and quiet. There are days of her glory, but subtly the golden dream crumbles, and a drowsy people have it dawn upon them that they are rudderless. The worms of worldliness have eaten infinitesimally small holes that draw water by seepage. But with a sudden bursting the seepage becomes a surge.

And as the water boils up into the hold, one hears the more-faint-every-minute cry of drowning rationality and spirituality.

Finally the cries die.

And the ship is left to the pirates of political entrenchment, who will stab, and cheat, and lie rather than give up the helm.

In other parts of the ship, the liberals allow the enemies of the faith aboard and realize their error too late—then plead for help.

But the pouting conservatives, having long ago stopped their ears to calls for communication, fail to hear . . .

. . . and, hating the liberals with such blind fury, fail to see the real enemies aboard . . .

. . . and as dusk settles upon the sea, the ship is taken.

It then becomes very quiet.

I gravely fear too-smooth soothsayers who, as Allen Drury says, "seem always to slide . . . between the sharp edges of clashing principles, and there find a glib, soft area of compromise that enervated all issues and sapped resolve."

There always seem to be those who chafe when a warning signal is put up. These well-meaning ninnies who evade the hatred some hold for us think we are the Apple of All Eyes.

But the Apple is too full of worms, such as worldly wisdom, half-truths, immature whim-following, the go-get'ums, and a dozen other wigglers.

If you think Christianity is completely adored, take a journey around the world, visit the places where men are not held in the context of Christian culture.

Ask them.

They'll tell you their honest feelings about the modern church's connection with vested interests, corrupt governments, and standing on the side of the Big Coin rather than Human Brokenness.

Ask them.

Jesus loved the tax collectors of his day. Ask the modern tax collector what he thinks of the church.

He'll tell you of millions of acres of tax-free land, dumping the resultant tax increase on the sore backs of the nation's Little People Who Foot the Bill.

Or question them about the big church businesses that ride without taxation and compete with "secular" business to sell the same products to the same customers.

This might explain to a bewildered clergy the Great Exodus of Executives from the modern denominations. In the minds of some of these executives, the church has lost its right to preach "Thou shalt not steal." . . .

. . . or "Thou shalt not covet another man's business."

It isn't really strange that tax collectors don't come to Jesus anymore.

Is it?

To accentuate our problem, after alienating the executives, losing the respect of government, we then finalize the agony by causing labor to question our concern.

Where, except in a few situations, has the church been the House of Brow Sweat?

There have been a few isolated cases where perspiration and inspiration have mixed.

Not isolated because the cases are few . . .

. . . but isolated because those who have shown concern have too often been equated with being spreaders of the bubonic plague.

But why villainize those who so strongly seem to care for those commoners whom Christ loved so well?

Time, commenting on the works of Richard O'Conner, says he ". . . does well with figures who never quite hit it big."

Christ has been specializing in "figures who never quite hit it big" for 193 decades.

Then why has the modern church so departed from the

spirit of Jesus that it considers ministers who specialize in those "figures who never quite hit it big" to be some sort of ordained Jimmy Hoffa?

Another group Jesus loved was the non-conformists. When Jesus was accused of hobnobbing with nondescripts, the most damning thing they could say was "he associates with . . . sinners."

A "sinner" in Jesus' day was not what our time would consider him to be. In the first century a sinner was a non-conformist, one who did not swallow hide, hair, and all the accepted forms of intrenched religiosity.

Jesus met the needs of these people and urged that one's non-conformity be dedicated to him. Our Lord was a switch-hitter without being a double-dealer.

The church must learn this or live in peril of extinction. But, too often, the church will crucify really creative non-conformity more rapidly than any other group in this static, thing-worshiping age.

Where, in any or all denominations, is there a comfortable home for the artist or dramatist?

Some denominations have encouraged these people of unique bent but always with paltry appropriations or grudging approval.

Probably the most constructive step in the Road Back would be for the church to make a giant effort to recapture the arts.

The art subjects in the latter sixteenth and early seventeenth centuries were more than ninety-five percent religious. Art subjects in the latter twentieth century are more than ninety-five percent secular. The secularization of art is almost complete.

In the later sixteenth century the artist was the church's

hero. In the latter part of the twentieth, he is the church's villain. If not the villain, he is—at best—ignored.

Few literary giants are claimed by the church. Faulkner, Hemingway, Eliot—none had anything for the church except mild contempt and certainly no loyalty.

The truth is that their creative brains were constantly harassed by most of the clergy.

The same can be said of the leading dramatists of the Tennessee Williams or Arthur Miller ilk and stamp.

One has the impression that all of the really creative minds think of the church as a Religious Scrooge, so they have cut off the conduit of conscience.

These men have a running love affair with their brains and the church hasn't the right to interfere with the romance if the church is as neurotic as they.

The clergy have grumbled everytime a play with a dirty word is written but their silence has been morgue-like when a profound moral is driven home.

I'll admit that some plays are about as aesthetic as a pig's bladder but a kindly, redemptive, Jesus-like church could have averted that.

Ecclesiastical power centers have been as self-contained as a house trailer, but there the comparison ends because house trailers are designed to go somewhere.

Certain clerics think they are the moral regulators of the universe, posing as a plutocracy of rule-setters.

But people stopped playing by the church-set rules when some really fresh Christian minds began to point out a few inconsistencies. These nonconformists were shot down in flames, of course; but not until their protests were heard.

If there can be some movement in the mausoleum there might be more resurrections than we think.

Blessed are the realistic, for they shall be called—and often.

These religious realists must continually believe that conscience must supersede the consensus.

The church has a future if it cordially and intelligently asserts its uniqueness. There is no future if it belligerently asserts its isolation.

We dare not become an electric blanket with no cord. We must plug in for power.

God has not given us a place of prominence to be used to bore the heaven out of everybody.

God never used a repetitious windbag to spark a reformation.

It is men of reverent candor, who are shocking, titillating, amusing and disturbing whom the masses follow.

But to be perfectly candid, such a man will discover some of the most gentle and charming headhunters, goaded by jealousy, hiding in every bush.

These are Religious Runts whose pious pituitary has been stunted because it is pickled in pharisaism. To every intelligent question they rebut with apocalyptic eccentricity.

The clergy must cease being led by men who are incarnated bombast, heaving masses of emotion, with more neuroses than they can handle.

Their motto is "To get along, go along."

A church, like a newspaper, can soon be out of date. When that happens, like the newspaper, it becomes good for nothing but wrapping fish that someone else has caught.

It becomes as superfluous as a wart . . . and twice as worrisome.

CHAPTER 12

Riding The Pulpit

Pat is a boy.

As such, anything short of going over Niagara Falls in a kayak is sheer boredom to him.

He had been bugging me to take him for a jaunt on our old Bahama Sloop.

Her name is "Sailbad the Sinner."

Not needing too much prodding on the matter, I yielded.

And I was glad I yielded because he didn't need to get out on those blue Atlantic waters one bit more than I did.

Sailbad looked as eager as she could, considering her arthritis. She suffered the rigors that every old sloop her age experiences: varicose rudder and badly in need of Lydia Sinkham.

It is a twenty-five minute trip from the Everglades dock to Palm Beach Inlet, the entrance into the open ocean.

As we neared the inlet I noticed Pat, straddling the pulpit. The pulpit is the very fore part of the boat, the bowsprit.

This was my son's favorite spot. He'd ridden up there every time we went out the inlet. The waves or swells were always just active enough to give him a mild dash of excitement.

Turning into the inlet I noticed it was much rougher than I had ever seen it.

The waves were about six feet and pipelining right in on us.

Suddenly I realized that Pat was still up front, riding the pulpit.

"Get back here, son!" I shouted into the wind.

He tried to obey me but it was too rough to let go.

So he just held on for his life.

A large wave hit the prow and sprayed me with a cold shower. Pat held on—but there were more and rougher waves ahead.

We were in real trouble.

I couldn't turn around in the narrow inlet—too many rocks and too little room. To turn around was to risk broaching.

And my only son was about to fall into a churning sea—without a life jacket.

He could be hurled into the big rocks or hit by sharks or barracuda.

One minute Pat would be fifteen feet in the air, his legs clamped around the bowsprit, his eyes wide in terror, his arms around the pulpit.

The next minute he would vanish from my sight, a hungry wave swallowing him. He would emerge from it, gasping for breath, nearly torn free from any grip on the boat.

I noticed his leg was bleeding profusely.

"O God, save my boy," I pleaded.

I turned the old boat toward jetties to relieve my son of

the wave action. But here was another problem. I would soon hit the giant rocks, dashing us to bits, if we continued on this new course.

The boat had to be turned into the big waves to make it out of the inlet to smoother waters.

Two or three of those big surly waves would get us to safe waters. My almost exhausted thirteen-year-old braced himself.

We took two of those Big Angries and the old boat made it out of the inlet.

Pat came off the pulpit as soon as he could, hugged the mast, gasping for breath.

Then he limped back to me. We embraced silently. He laid down on the deck, and shielded his eyes with his arm. I could see his heart beating, his naked chest glistening and dripping wet.

After a few minutes of rest, he opened his eyes and said something his preacher father will never forget.

"Dad, I never knew it was so rough, riding the pulpit."

My son wasn't the only person to make that discovery.

From the day Simon Peter mounted the rostrum and became the fiery-eyed prophet of Pentecost's pulpit until last Sunday it has always been a rough, exciting ride.

Did you ever think of the fact that the pulpit in the church is named for the pulpit of a ship?

A most interesting comparison can be made between the old-time pulpit riders of the giant schooners that once proudly plowed the seas and the man who regularly preaches in your pulpit every Sunday.

The ship's pulpit served several purposes.

The first use of the pulpit was *to warn the crew of submerged danger.*

This is the purpose of the church's pulpit riders today.

What are some of the dangers lurking just beneath the surface?

Look out for a submerged log that could ram the prow of the Ship of Zion. It is called *isolationism.* . . .

We can worship the past to the degree that we forget the future.

We can worship our exclusiveness so much as to be repudiated by the lost world outside.

We cannot strut arrogantly and blindly in a smog of smugness. This always leads to pharisaism.

God never called us to be dour judges, standing in the robes of prudery . . . we are in the business of redemptive involvement—not hyper-righteous investigation.

Modern Christians must realize that we are in sales—not management. The management of the affairs of men belongs to God Himself.

The Father, Son, and Holy Spirit are saying, "Leave the driving to Us."

Somehow we have been led to believe that we are to wage a private war with the Evil One, forgetting that the battle is the Lord's.

We can fight all alone but relativism, scientism, and neo-atheism will methodically pull our teeth, making us look old before our time.

We cannot toothlessly gum the devil and expect him to writhe in agony.

Let us ask the Divine Dentist to give us a new set of teeth.

He'll give us our bite back.

There is nothing so harmless as a toothless, flabby, nice old punch-drunk has-been denomination. All he is used for is to sweep out the gym—while somebody else—bristling, quick, and disciplined steals the headlines of the press and the heartlines of the people.

We do have a fight on our hands. And we can win—because, as Ethel Waters told Virginia Seelig, "Honey, Jesus don't sponsor no flops!" We must slug it out with racism—from the Ku Klux Klan to the Black Muslims.

The battle lines must be drawn with institutionalized evil: gambling, alcoholism, governmental corruption, divorce, ministerial gossip-mongering, divisiveness in America and all such powers that despise the human spirit.

If you do this you will discover how rough it is riding the pulpit.

But, dig your spurs in and ride, because we have on our hands a dry-eyed church in a hell-bound world.

And we cannot win if we pit a lukewarm church against a burning paganism.

Many a ship has been sent to the bottom by another lurking danger to the good Lord's church.

It is *ministerial jealousy.*

There is nothing more shocking to the unconverted world than to discover that jealousy is the stock-in-trade of too many ministers.

The unconverted would become completely disillusioned if they really knew how vicious a virus this is.

If I have ever raised a warning flag before our preachers, I am doing it now.

Remember Dr. W. W. Adams' searching, winnowing message in which he said it was not the liberal-conservative conflict that shattered the then Northern Baptist Convention. I won't ever forget that faithful old prophet warning us that jealousy can shatter a denomination.

While we are taking some strong positions on important issues, let us come out against ministerial green-eyed gossip.

A man who evidences such a lack of Christian love and New Testament fellowship has no business preaching Jesus. A person who cannot be trusted to tell the truth about a fellow minister cannot be trusted to tell the truth about God.

You gossip about a brother or sister in Christ and it will come back to you.

As Jerri Southern sings, "Things You Do Come Back To You As Though They Knew The Way."

As James Cole pointed out in one of his great editorials:
"I feel sorry for the guys
Who criticize and minimize
The other guys
Whose enterprise
Has made them rise
Above the guys
Who criticize and minimize."

One giant hidden reef is the very real danger of *governmental control*.

There are among us some semi-sanctified simpletons who are more interested in what our government wants than what the New Testament teaches.

Some in our own circles are advocating direct taxation of our church houses.

I want to urge our great government to take a long look at history before they tie in with some ecclesiastical politicism.

Historically, if church and state are separate, the church is the pillar of the state; if church and state are merged, the church is the caterpillar of the state—it eats the vitals out of it.

Let others do it if they think they must but we weren't born to be put on some government's political what-not shelf.

If we allow the state to take over the church or the church to take over the state, we should change our name to the Southern Barnacle Convention, a group that has affixed itself to the Ship of State—and is taking a free ride.

Gentlemen, it isn't free. It is the most costly ride we'll ever take.

Our task is not to take a free ride on the Ship of State.

Our task is to ride the pulpit on the Ship of Zion.

We got where we are by being what we are. If we compromise ourselves out of the right-to-prophecy, we will be splendid. . . .

. . . and blended.

Baptists and Presbyterians have had a love affair with American ideals longer than anyone else. Let those who came about their so-called convictions late give them up early. Let us who came about our deep convictions early give them up *never!*

It is more important that we keep the right to be heard than anything else.

In the names of Smyth, Helwys, Williams, Leland, Carey, and Truett, I beg you, my brothers, remember who-you-are, how-you-got-here, where-you-came-from, what-you-believe . . . if you tend to these factors, where-you-are-going will take care of itself.

Another not-so-submerged big rock is *ecumenicism.*

We are constantly hearing that America is decaying.

I am completely incapable of judging if this be true.

But of one thing I am convinced: That great denominations have been diverted from the great commission of evangelism to the great confusion of ecumenicism.

Whole denominations are wasting their energies being on-the-verge-with-an-urge-to-merge when they should be using their vitality to convert men to Christ.

Evangelism will do what ecumenicalism will never accomplish.

Let us clarify to the people that we do not mean to imply a lack of love for Christians of other groups—we simply believe that denominational variety breeds more spiritual creativity.

We believe biblical conviction is superior to the compromises of unionism.

We aren't afraid of dialogue but it must be discussion as equals instead of "separated brethren."

There is a truly wonderful aspect to remaining cordially and cooperatively separate. The tragedy is that this is misunderstood by the world outside and some within our own ranks.

We are pictured to the world as not believing in the family of man, as believing we are superior to all other Christians; when in reality we do believe in the family of man so much that we warn all mankind of the dangers of a weakened superchurch that preaches a syncretistic semigospel.

Stand by this and your pulpit ride will be rough—and glorious.

You must lean out of your pulpit and peer through the morning fog if you're going to see the next submerged danger, *pseudo-intellectualism.*

We have heard these sad, sick sophists preach. They begin by apologizing for being limited by the church, the Bible, and the Gospel, then proceed to preach a kind of gastro in-

testinal hiccup about relevance. They criticize Bible
believers for being irrelevant, then demonstrate just how
relevant their message is by speaking for twelve minutes on
the topic, "The Socio-Eco-Politico-Religio Factors In God's
Decision to Support the Viet Cong."

"Don't embarrass us by preaching about salvation," they
plead. "Speak on some relevant issue like the recent cheese
strikes in Luxembourg."

There is nothing more unbecoming than a cynical
preacher.

Why is it that so many seminary graduates seem almost
unanimously to be cynical young punks who are better at
winning arguments than building people?

These are the kind who make you wish birth control were
retroactive.

These young cynics never seem to realize that the chip on
their shoulder, and their head, is one and the same.

If someone asks them how to be saved they become as
clumsy as a chimpanzee with chopsticks.

If they ever take over the denominations, we'll move
about as fast as a retarded glacier—only colder.

They will make the church of the Lord a hangout for social
workers—important as social work is. But, remember, social
consciousness must be the *result* of the new birth, not a sop
for the conscience of a backslidden preacher who substi-
tutes social work for a gospel he no longer believes.

We must take an intelligent, spiritual approach to facing
the social issues of our time. Many are attempting to get us
to take a strong stand on capital punishment. Let us not be
like the lady in West Palm Beach who told me she was vio-
lently opposed to capital punishment, especially for children
because it might do them permanent damage.

Let us be socially aware—and intelligent about it.

For years we have listened to liberal Protestants chide with the demand, "Get relevant."

Now I want to stare right back into their faces and insist, "Get reverent."

When will you become reverent before the Scriptures . . . Is it your sole authority?

If not, what is?

When will you become reverent about the deity of Jesus Christ?. . . Do you believe Him to be the Way, the Truth, and the Life?

If not, how is man saved?

Don't stutter, don't philosophize, don't vaporize!

How is man saved?

If you can't explain simply how a man is saved in the shortest sentences and the clearest terms, then you are the one who is irrelevant.

You are irrelevant and irreverent.

May God forgive you for compounding the spiritual ignorance of our decadent era.

If one lonely preacher plants himself firmly on the New Testament and there abides, the world may not appreciate the preacher or remember his name; but it will be drawn closer to the cross. . . .

. . . and that is what preachers are for.

Still another of the important purposes of riding a boat's pulpit is *to seek out the best fishing spots.*

This is also the purpose of riding the church pulpit.

What must we do to be the best fishermen possible?

This is, after all, the most important question before us.

There are several factors to be considered in searching for the best places to fish for men.

We are overly freighted with too much stowage which we simply must throw overboard.

1. Let us throw overboard excessive busyness with lesser activities.

Frankly, my people are often too tired to witness. The Royal Canadian Exercise Program requires no more use of energy than to be a loyal member of the average church.

I feel like a bugler with a bruised lip sounding reveille every few hours calling our people to some "bold new program."

Many church members have been seriously injured in a "crash program."

They say in heaven there are no partings. Honestly, I find myself hoping there will be no meetings!

Many of our leaders are concerned about the fact that we waste too much energy on too many battlefronts.

Let us narrow it down to some old-fashioned personal evangelism.

A church that isn't evangelistic isn't a church.

A church that ceases to be evangelistic will cease to be evangelical and missionary.

There is no use taking a lamp to Indonesia that won't burn at home.

A church that ceases to be evangelistic will be a divided church.

Brethren, cease your feuding—and fish!

It is difficult to be interested in witnessing if all your energy is wasted in a Deacons' meeting, which too often is a long hot ride through ulcer gulch . . .

. . . or a finance committee conference, if it is like a conference with the Smothers Brothers, who are the self-styled "watchdogs of the budget" and are mad about it.

More church feuds are solved by evangelism than this world dreams of.

You can't fish and fight at the same time. You must neglect your net or your gun.

May your pulpit become a miniature Calvary where you die a little bit to see men saved.

For every sermon there should be a drop of your own fresh blood.

2. Let us throw overboard the image of Victorian prudery.

You and I know that we are a happy Christian fellowship but we can't get enough fellows in the ship because we have been depicted by our interpreters as serious old guilt collectors, able to hear a sin drop a mile away.

Man suffers from being overly baked in the hot oven of cynicism and frozen to death in the chilling refrigerator of non-involvement.

A hot-collared sermon on the sin of playing solitaire will miss him by a light-year.

We must not be a terror for sinners but a haven for them.

We preach against the limbo of liberal looseness without considering the purgatory of pharisaical prudery.

There is need for us to understand that the cause of the "new morality" is disillusionment with the promises of the old morality.

All we have heard is that America can be saved by being a moral nation.

It simply isn't true.

The only hope for saving America is a new surge of old spirituality.

Spirituality is morality plus.

Plus what?

Plus a personal relationship with God in Christ.

Plus flaming, witnessing Christians.

As Paul says, "Having begun in the Spirit, will you be made perfect in the flesh?"

An effort to be moral always ends in failure.

The thrust is missing.

And all merely moral movements die on the launching pad of good intentions.

Let us tell the world that we are happy adventurers—not moral umpires.

3. We must throw overboard the heresy that the church house is the best place to witness.

In fact, a pretty good case can be made that it is the poorest place to witness.

C. E. Autrey is right in urging us to give the church a chance to breathe by going outside.

Billy Graham is right and has the packed stadium to prove it.

Remember, it is the Sermon on the Mount—not the Sermon in the Cathedral.

Has there ever been a major national awakening that took place inside church buildings?

The people sang Luther's "A Mighty Fortress" in the streets.

The Welch revivals burst forth—in the mines.

Wesley preached—from his father's tombstone.

Finney's revival—began in a schoolhouse.

Moody preached—in civic arenas.

Let's give the Gospel air!

To summarize:

If we do away with excessive busyness with lesser activities;

If we throw overboard the image of Victorian prudery;

If we rid ourselves of the concept that the church house is the best place to witness;

And pray until we are filled with the Holy Spirit;

We can fish anywhere and the nets will be loaded and overtaxed.

There is another important fishing technique.

When will we face up to the fact that, important as it is, preaching will not convert the world. Pulpit preaching must have added to it personal witnessing.

At present we are suffering from a pretty bad case of Logorrhea—a severe running off of the mouth.

The average sermon contains 6,000 words. The average pastor preaches three sermons a week. That is 18,000 words every seven days. Multiply the number of pastors by 18,000 words.

That is how many hundreds of millions of words a week? If pulpit preaching without personal witnessing could win the world, we would have converted every man, mammal, fish, and fowl a long time ago.

Logorrhea!

That's our sickness.

We dare not be a babbling talkocrat who is the verbal equivalent of the fifty-mile hike.

I am a failure as a preacher if I cannot personally win someone to Christ.

"If every saved one won one,

And each one won, won one,

What hosts would be won,

When everyone won, had won one."

The final purpose of the pulpit prow is *to take the shock of the big waves first to make the ride easier for the rest of the ship.*

Let us not fear a collision with reality. That is the one place the Lord will be.

Let us not seek uncritical acceptance. That is the one place the Lord will not be.

We can drift out on the waves of adulation and find the current of the applause of self-orientated congregations has carried us so far out that we can never make it back to the shore of reality.

The carnal way to save our lives is to never risk them.

The spiritual way is to see the churning flood of human hatred, hurl ourselves into it, knowing that Christ promised we would surface again after the wave was dead.

O God, make our pulpit riders to be what Dag Hammarskjold described:

> "Smiling, sincere, incorruptible
> His body disciplined and limber.
> A man who had become what he could,
> And was what he was—
> Ready at any moment to gather everything
> Into one simple sacrifice."

May God make that a description of every pastor!

There are whirlpools that can suck you under. Every minute is surrounded by a dozen dizzy isms, appearing beautiful, like busy prisms—which, if followed, will result in a lovely multi-hued religious nothing.

If you follow these false ways and much later die of soul rot, many may weep at your grave—including the devil.

To avoid this you must learn to live with sneering epithets. . . .

. . . such as "peculiar."

The culture vultures will try to knock off your rough edges.

They will attempt to give you some cliches to hide behind.

Be sure they will damn you if you do not yield to their mesmerizing way.

Sit tight in your pulpit.

Remember Jeremiah 1:17, "Thou therefore gird up thy loins, and arise, and speak unto them all that I command thee: be not dismayed at their faces, lest I confound thee before them."

If you do this you will discover just how rough it is riding the pulpit.

The big waves will pipeline in on you.

Some of us will not survive the storm.

But you'll be in good company.

O, I think I hear the clapping of nail-scarred hands!

Remember . . . Remember . . .

. . . Dietrich Bonhoeffer, up front, riding the pulpit?

The angry, churning wave of Nazism came charging at the Ship of Zion. Just before the monster hit the ship, Bonhoeffer screamed into the wind, "Jesus invited us, come with me . . . and die!"

The pulpit and the prow vanished under the dark wave. The whole ship shuddered . . .

. . . every passenger felt the shock of it.

Suddenly, the pulpit burst up out of the wave.

Bonhoeffer was gone.

. . . but the old Ship of Zion . . .

. . . sailed on.

Bonhoeffer died . . .

. . . but so did Nazism.

I think I hear the clapping of nail-scarred hands.

Remember . . . Remember . . .

. . . Bill Wallace, up front riding the pulpit?

The angry, churning waves of communism came charging at the Ship of Zion.

Just before the monster hit the ship, we saw silent Bill hanging on with all the strength he had . . .

. . . The pulpit and the prow vanished under the dark wave. The whole ship shuddered . . .

. . . Every passenger felt the shock of it.

Suddenly, the pulpit burst up out of the wave.

Our Bill was gone . . .

. . . but the old Ship of Zion . . .

. . . sailed on.

Bill Wallace died . . .

. . . and as sure as there is a God in heaven . . .

. . . so will communism.

I think I hear the clapping of nail-scarred hands.

Remember . . . Remember . . .

My brother, today you are riding the pulpit.

The angry, churning waves of Secular-Cityism . . . God is Dead-ism and Honest-to-God-ism are charging in on you.

Just before the monster hits the ship, get a good grip on your pulpit.

Your pulpit and prow will vanish under the dark wave. The whole ship will shudder—everyone of your passengers will feel the shock of it.

Suddenly, your pulpit will burst out of the wave.

You will be gone . . .

. . . but the Old Ship of Zion . . .

. . . will sail on because of you . . .

. . . sail on . . .

    . . . and on . . .

        . . . and on!